Growing Up
GODLESS

Growing Up
GODLESS

A Parent's Guide to
Raising Kids without Religion

DEBORAH MITCHELL

Foreword by Dale McGowen,
author of *Parenting Beyond Belief*

STERLING ETHOS
New York

STERLING ETHOS
New York

An Imprint of Sterling Publishing
387 Park Avenue South
New York, NY 10016

ISBN 978-1-4549-1098-5

Distributed in Canada by Sterling Publishing
c/o Canadian Manda Group, 165 Dufferin Street
Toronto, Ontario, Canada M6K 3H6
Distributed in the United Kingdom by GMC Distribution Services
Castle Place, 166 High Street, Lewes, East Sussex, England BN7 1XU
Distributed in Australia by Capricorn Link (Australia) Pty. Ltd.
P.O. Box 704, Windsor, NSW 2756, Australia

For information about custom editions, special sales, and premium and
corporate purchases, please contact Sterling Special Sales at 800-805-5489
or specialsales@sterlingpublishing.com.

Manufactured in the United States of America

2 4 6 8 10 9 7 5 3 1

www.sterlingpublishing.com

FOR MY MOTHER,

who still teaches me to always have faith
and to never stop believing.

"I cannot conceive of a god who rewards and punishes his creatures or has a will of the kind that we experience in ourselves. Neither can I—nor would I want to—conceive of an individual that survives his physical death. Let feeble souls, from fear or absurd egotism, cherish such thoughts. I am satisfied with the mystery of the eternity of life and a glimpse of the marvelous structure of the existing world, together with a devoted striving to comprehend a portion, be it ever so tiny, of the Reason that manifests itself in nature."

—Albert Einstein

Contents

RITUALS AND HOLIDAYS

IN THE COMMUNITY

LESSONS LEARNED

Foreword

by Dale McGowan

I n autumn of 2005, I floated the idea of a book on nonreligious parenting to my agent. He said he wasn't convinced there was a market for such a thing, but he was willing to shop it around to publishers.

Unfortunately, most of the publishers said the same thing. When asked why they thought there was no market, their reasoning was impeccable:

"If there were a market, there would already be books for it."

I was stunned. I wasn't trying to convince them to publish *Antique Dental Drill Collecting for Left-handed Capricorns*. I was proposing a title aimed at the fastest-growing belief segment in the United States. Even conservative estimates suggested that the population of nonreligious Americans had grown to about 40 million by that time (about 12 percent of the overall population), and no fewer than 8–10 million were raising children without religion. But they were doing so with virtually no published resources, largely because publishers saw the lack of existing books as a reason not to publish new ones.

Contrast this with a dozen major titles on Jewish parenting, despite the fact that only about 2 percent of the U.S. population (roughly 6.5 million people) identifies as Jewish.

Eventually, we did find a publisher for *Parenting Beyond Belief*. It became one of their best-selling titles ever, along with the 2009 sequel, *Raising Freethinkers*. Nonreligious parenting was finally on the map.

Since then, there's been an explosion of secular parenting blogs, websites, discussion boards, and local groups. But aside from Andrew Parks's *Between a Church and a Hard Place*, a unique personal narrative, we've gone back to almost complete radio silence on the bookshelves.

That's why I was delighted to hear about *Growing Up Godless*, Deborah Mitchell's thoughtful and intelligent addition to the conversation. Though there is overlap, our approaches are not identical. She covers many of the same issues I've addressed but brings a fresh perspective, new angles, and different solutions. There are the same struggles with parental objectivity, grappling with morality and mortality, extended family, helping kids deal with pressure from religious peers, and generally helping the family find its way in a religiously inflected world.

Nonreligious parents tend to read skeptically. They aren't looking for authoritative pronouncements to follow word for word; they're looking for ideas and suggestions from people who've encountered the same issues and thought carefully about them. They aren't confused by differences of approach. On the contrary, it gives them more options to consider, which is always a good thing.

Of course, it's also great to see the ways in which our approaches are hand-in-glove, like our shared enthusiasm for the idea of teaching religion in schools—one that tends to raise quite a few atheist eyebrows. And Deborah's reasons for liking the idea are right in sync with my own. It has to be done right, of course, and that's a tall order. But it's not a coincidence that the UK has religious education in schools and is highly secular, while Americans can be breathtakingly ignorant of the tenets of even their own religions, not to mention other religions—and tend to be deeply faithful. Knowledge is a good thing.

So welcome to the secular parenting bookshelf, Deborah. Here's to adding even more voices in the years to come.

Dale McGowan

A Disclaimer

I live in a glass house. I know some will throw stones. When I see inconsistencies or absurdities in the God narrative, I write about them, but I realize that I can also be inconsistent and absurd, too. My kids started off on a diet of religion. I thought that was the right thing to do. Then I changed my mind, and changed my parenting tactics. I've tried my best. That's all any of us can do, whether we are believers or not. We all want to raise good, healthy, self-sufficient, and content kids. I know that, in spite of our differences in belief systems, we share this very important goal.

Sometimes I stereotype. Sometimes I generalize. We all do. It's a way of understanding, of connecting the knowledge we have with the world we are living in. I judge believers, just as they judge me. Believers must think: How can she do that? Doesn't she know any better? Her children will grow up without morals. She is yanking hope right out from under her kids. And *I* wonder how adults who believe can leap the chasm of reason; how they can believe things that don't even make sense. They are pulling the proverbial wool over their kids' eyes, controlling them with the hope and fear religion inculcates.

I claim to be raising kids as independent, logical thinkers, independent of religious dogma. Of course, those who believe can be critical thinkers, too, but in order to be a card-carrying member of a religious organization, you have to accept unrealistic beliefs without question. And if you question, you still have to accept your doubts anyway if you want to retain your membership. It seems to me a small part of your brain has to be switched off, the same part that tells you goblins and vampires and Santa aren't real.

I call myself humanist. You may be Christian. Or Muslim. Or Jewish. I sometimes lean toward atheism in my certainty that there is no God. We haven't been abandoned by an angry supreme being on this planet; we've just always been alone. I sometimes think, perhaps there was some sort of force that deliberately created life. I can neither prove nor disprove that possibility. I don't call myself atheist because the certainty of believing there is no higher intelligence seems just as rigid as the evangelical who swears to know there is a God. Sometimes, I just think, Wouldn't it be nice if someone or something benevolent *were* out there, watching over us, just waiting to embrace us after we die? But I always think, the story we have about this version of God and his son, Jesus—that's just a projection of us. We've created one of the greatest narratives of all times, pieced together with thousands of years of short stories, folktales, and parables.

My way is neither right nor wrong. Neither is yours. For this reason, what I do believe in is this: Where our circles overlap and our lives intersect, we should keep our views about the existence of God tucked away just as we would our undergarments.

Peace.

Introduction

'll be honest with you. For a large part of my life, I was not really honest about who I am. For twenty years, I remained silent and just nodded when people talked to me about God. When asked to pray, I bowed my head but did not speak. Sometimes, I'd mouth the words so people thought I was participating, when I was really thinking, "Why can't I just tell them I don't believe?" When I received e-mails to forward about angels and God, I immediately hit the delete key and hoped no one would ask me why I didn't send it on to ten more friends. When acquaintances or coworkers would ask me what church I belonged to, I hemmed and hawed and said I sometimes went to my local Catholic church. And when my dad passed away, people told me that heaven was a better place with him in it. Of course, those people didn't know that my father had his doubts, too, and that he liked living here on earth with the people he loved. What better place could there be?

When I moved to Texas, I realized how influential religion could be in our day-to-day lives. Religion is big business. We have the most megachurches in the country, and in my city of 130,000 people, not far from Dallas, every few blocks there's a church. Cars, clothes, and human skin are marked with crosses and fish symbols and Bible verses. People "get in your business" about religion, and in my town, it's the Baptists who rule.

Don't get me wrong. I like people, no matter what their faith or lack of it. There are good and bad apples everywhere. I'm not singling out the Baptists, but in this city, their influence and reach is impressive. They train their children to evangelize in the schools and to their friends of other beliefs. As part of their member commitment, they must agree, among other things, to "invite the unchurched to attend." Their mission, as stated on their website, is to save lost or fallen souls and "return them to God." That means it's open season on those of us who don't go to church, who don't even believe in God—and they don't care if you don't want their advances. They'll press on. You'll soon realize that you're not a person with your own views; you're just a really big fish. And if they get you in their net, they'll get a big notch in their "I'm going to heaven" belt.

It was this frustration that inspired me to start a blog in the early 2000s called Kids without Religion. The blog became a good place to meet other parents who were also raising kids without religion, although early on, there were not many of us. Dale McGowan, who wrote *Parenting Beyond Belief*, was the only other parent I knew at the time writing and blogging about this topic.

In 2006, out of frustration over what I had seen in my sons' schools, I decided to write a column for the *Dallas Morning News* about teaching all religions in schools as a comparative religious studies class. There were people who agreed with me, and a lot of people who didn't. Then there were people who only wanted Christianity taught in schools—oh, and they wanted to take me back to God where I belonged, just as soon as I was ready.

Around that time, I also saw a wave of atheist men come onto the scene, and a few years later, a couple of female voices. But the voice that was still missing was that of a mom. Moms and Dads are really on the front lines of the next generation of churchgoers or, in our case, the "unchurched." We don't pray at the dinner table, but we are thankful. We don't discuss Bible verses, but we do discuss the history of religion. We teach our kids to question the status quo. We drive our kids to soccer games and doctors' appointments; we ask them about their friends and talk to them about our values. We are cultivating a new crop, and we've been growing our kids without religion behind closed doors for years. With the rise of the Nones, the religiously unaffiliated, along with the children we are raising, there will be a lot more parents like us out there in the next couple of decades.

As an agnostic, I had become frustrated with being in the proverbial closet, and I wanted to share my perspective—our perspective—as parents and nonbelievers. I wanted to dispel the myths that we—you and I—are amoral or are agents of the Devil. Our views count.

A few years passed before I decided to write a column for CNN.com called, "Why I Raise My Kids without God," which became the most viewed and the most commented citizen's report on CNN.com. Although there are still a lot of people who want to scream at and shame and convert us, I found that there are a lot of parents raising kids without religion—many more than I had ever suspected—who wanted to step out of the shadows. We are tired of the polarization and the religious fever that dominates so much of our culture, and we just want to bring respect, tolerance, and kindness to our national dialogue.

There are a lot of extreme voices on both sides, but I hope that I am not and will never be one of them. Though I may criticize religion's inconsistencies or hypocrisies, I don't want to shame or embarrass those who believe in God, whether they have a particular religious affiliation or not. Belief brings many people hope, structure, and comfort, and I don't want to take that away from anyone, especially those I care about. The path to change is not made by forcing those who believe to give up their God or by mocking a belief system. Change is made by pulling up a chair at America's religious round table and asking that our voices be heard and our views accepted.

We do not wish to be conquests—we've given our stance a lot of reasoned thought. We've read the Bible, studied the history of religion, and sat in the pews prior to making our decisions. One of the biggest frustrations about coming out of the religious closet is that many believers think that we are just unchurched or unlearned—if we could only understand "the truth," we'd change our minds and believe. This, it seems, is the kindling for many angry arguments.

The best we can hope for is that we all respect each other's views. I realize that, in questioning long-held religious beliefs, the arguments against the existence of God are oftentimes condescending. We assume that reason should rule; a believer's faith is trampled under arguments of science and logic, ignoring the fact that faith means believing in things none of us understands. How did we get here? Why are we here? What created the material that made the universe?

Perhaps, as nonbelievers, we inadvertently attack the business model of our nation's churches; we say they have a flawed product—a God that doesn't deliver, one that doesn't offer church members a return on their investment of time and money. Perhaps there is fear that nonbelievers will cause churches to lose customers. These are valid concerns.

On the other hand, believers are quick to point out that they have a right to (according to their government) and are commanded to (according to their God) spread the Word of God. Nonbelievers, in asking for religion-free public spaces, take away the ability to evangelize and to recruit new church members. "I was brought up by my church to evangelize," I've heard some say. "It's part of who I am." Yes, there are many personal things we learn growing up that make us who we are: habits, values, language. We learn that spanking is acceptable—or not acceptable. We think our ways and our preferences are the best, but we don't force them on strangers; we don't insist that they adopt our preferences as their own.

The conflict between the haves (those who have God) and the have-nots in this country is something we can reconcile. You and I are united with our neighbors by our country, our humanity, our history, by the air we breathe, and by the water we drink. We are sharing the same experience on this planet at the same time in its history. We share consciousness. Regardless of our preferences and the beliefs we hold invisibly and inextricably inside us, there should be room for us to meet mutually and respectfully in the middle. Believers don't want us to use science to poke at their faith? We don't want them to tell us that our godlessness is the cause of crime in this country. We won't fear their belief if they don't fear our lack of it. Nor will we try to recruit them to our side, and we ask that they not try to recruit us. We are a rising demographic, and our nation must find a way to peacefully embrace all of our worldviews.

Nonbelievers do not want to take religion out of homes and churches; we do not want to separate our neighbors' faith from their families. We only want to untangle God from the public sphere. Why don't we agree to keep our beliefs—or nonbelief—in our minds and our hearts in public? Why don't we agree to treat each other with kindness, respect, and tolerance so that our children can grow up and feel valued, no matter what they believe about God?

This book is about raising respectful, tolerant, enlightened kids with good boundaries. I hope you find support and encouragement to stay the course. I also hope these essays make you realize that you are not alone, that there is a growing community of nonbelievers out there—people just like you and me who simply want to do the right thing and raise good children.

THINGS
∙ TO ∙
LEARN

Raising Kids
without Religion

What does it mean to raise kids without religion? It means that, when kids ask why they shouldn't lie or why they should talk to the kid who is being bullied, you tell them "because it's the right thing to do, because you make the world a better place by doing the right thing." When you take God and religion out of the picture, you place responsibility onto the shoulders of your children. No, you tell your kids, you won't go to heaven, but you can sleep better at night. You will make your family proud. You will feel good about who you are. When we help others "because God wants us to," we do not necessarily do it because we want to. Rather, we have a prize in mind: God's approval, which translates into life everlasting. I suppose that morality backed by God is not a bad thing, but it can be a weak system. Take, for example, all the corruption and abuse in Catholicism over the centuries. If you need proof that religion doesn't produce moral followers, just look to the many churches caught up in scandals.

When you raise your children without religion, you don't tell them, "This was God's plan for you." I think that telling children the big guy in the sky has a special path for them makes children narcissistic; it makes them think the world is at their disposal and that, no matter what happens, it doesn't really matter because God is in control. That gives kids a false sense of security and engenders selfishness. "No matter what I do, God loves me and forgives me."

When you raise kids without religion, you tell them the truth—while you are special to Mom and Dad, you are not special to the rest of the world. You are just a very, very small part of a big machine. Whether that machine is nature or society, the influence you have is minute. No matter how important you think you are, the truth is, you're not. In the bigger picture, no one is important. The realization of your insignificance gives you a true sense of humbleness.

When you tell your children there is no God, they begin to understand that the family and friends around them are all they have, so they'd better treat them well. People depend on them.

When you tell your children there is no God, they get a sense of immediacy, of how important and precious their time on this planet is. Yes, life is truly a gift. *Blessed* and *lucky* are interchangeable terms. They mean the same thing. You were damn lucky to be born and to be healthy and to have a life full of people who love and care for you.

When you tell your children there is no God and something bad happens, they don't ask why God let this happen to them (after all, God loves them and how could *he* hurt them like this?). They understand that bad things happen and sometimes there is no reason. Tough luck. A bad break. Or, perhaps they see some sort of connection. X happened because of Y. But sometimes things just happen that are out of their control.

When you raise your kids without religion, your children learn that one religion or God(s), past or present, is no better or worse than another. They are all connected, all variations of the same stories that have been told since humans were able to imagine God. They all have their strengths and their weaknesses.

When you raise your kids without religion, they understand that babies are not "gifts" from God but products of a relationship. Their bodies are temples, and they are temporary, so treat them with respect. They don't picket Planned Parenthood because aborting a fetus is not their choice to make for someone else.

When you raise kids without religion or God, they learn that they are both fragile and strong. Fragile because circumstances in life may turn their lives upside down at any time; strong because, in spite of many adversities, humans can still survive and thrive.

How to Find Me
in Heaven: My Big Lie

A t four years old, one of my sons was very interested in heaven and the afterlife. One Thursday morning in spring, as we were planting geraniums in our flowerbeds, he asked, "Mommy?"

Yes?

"After we die, we're buried in the ground, right?"

Yes, I told him. I had wondered what he was thinking as he quietly dug holes.

"Do they put dirt over your face?"

Sort of, I said. *They bury you in a coffin, in a nice box.* I didn't want to get into the gory details of death with my four-year-old, no matter how precocious he was. There's nothing more heartbreaking than telling your kid that he's going to die one day, that his amazing body that can do so many things will one day be nothing more than a useless vessel, which will break down and blow away, just like the papery wings of a butterfly.

A few minutes went by as we worked silently side by side, pulling the tender roots out of flimsy flowerpots and transplanting them with the greatest care. I could almost feel my kid thinking about what I had told him.

"Mommy?" he said again. "Do we die with our eyes open or closed?"

Closed, I told him, to make it easier to digest.

"Then you can't see anything," he said.

That's right, I told him, *but you are dead, so you can't see anything anyway.* I wondered if he was trying to understand what it meant to die, if he'd suddenly understood his own mortality.

"Then how will I find you in heaven?"

I felt a lump in my throat as I was caught off guard. It was a rare moment for me. I realized that my son was truly disturbed by something that he was just beginning to understand: death, separation, finality. He was struggling not to cry, too. Even now, as I write this, I feel that lump and fight back emotion. I didn't tell him the truth then about what I believed, and it was the last time I ever lied to him. At that moment, I just wanted his young mind to find comfort, so I told him the spirit has a way of finding people it loves, though I had no more belief in what I said than I did in Casper the ghost.

My son was satisfied and did not question God and heaven again for several more months. I understood with that conversation why so many parents need religion. It was hard enough for me to know that one day my son would be buried in the very earth he was digging up, buried, perhaps, for all eternity. It was painful to think that the child I loved so intensely with every cell in me, the one I made out of my blood and bones and set free into the world, would one day be gone.

Nothingness is a hard concept to wrap your mind around, even when you're an adult. I'm sure I'm not the only parent who has struggled with what to tell children about dying. Belief in God does provide a safety net of sorts, an emotional security that life and death are seamless and continual. And, as a nonbeliever, you realize that they *are* seamless and continual, just in a different way. The star stuff that makes us who we are will go back to being star stuff again.

Big Questions
and Little Kids

When my older child was younger, he went to a Christian preschool and kindergarten. In my town, there were no other choices at the time for good preschool programs, and, really, I didn't mind exposing my child to religion. Every week, the kids had chapel time where, for thirty minutes, the children would sit tidily in the pews and listen to a child-friendly sermon. The pastor used a troll doll to represent Jesus. Yeah, how ironic, using an imaginary character with screaming-orange hair to represent another imaginary character who can turn water into wine, but you'd be surprised how much kids talk about Jesus when they think of him as a little troll. A visible representation of God's son was much easier to relate to when presented as a tangible, smiling toy doll.

It was also during my son's preschool years that I started being forthright with him about my religious views. When he asked me who made God, I didn't tell him, as I was taught, that God always was and always will be. That didn't make sense to me, and I'm sure it wouldn't make sense to a kid. So I just told my son that I didn't know. At that time, I gave him simple responses—not complex answers, just responses.

He was still pondering the "Who made God" question as we drove down the highway one afternoon, and a few minutes later he said, "Maybe God made himself. Or a machine did. And if a machine made him, then who made the machine? Because someone had to make the machine." You can see how the idea of God throws even preschoolers into an infinite loop. If God made us, who made God? And that person? And the person before that? It's the endless mirror effect; the same image, like the same question, goes on and on and on forever. No end and no beginning.

There's always the problem as a nonbeliever that you cannot explain how *anything* came into existence: the ingredients for the Primordial Soup or for the Big Bang. When you start reversing gears and thinking back, back, back to what existed before the Big Bang, you begin to wonder if you're even real. You almost expect your brain to collapse in on itself like a dying star. The thing is, no matter how much we try, humans will probably never know what came before our universe.

Carl Sagan gave us a beautiful way to think of our recent arrival here. He said, "Because the cosmos is also within us. We're made of star-stuff. We are a way for the cosmos to know itself." It is comforting in a sense to think of ourselves as offspring of the universe, where one day, we will be returned, set free from the confines of the body and spread throughout the cosmos like a sneeze—or even seeds for some new organism. An awareness of this helps us see Mother Nature as a friend to be respected and cared for, not as a foe to be used and conquered.

From there, it was easy to teach my kid not to leave the water running while brushing his teeth. *We don't want to take too much water from the pond down the street and harm the fish,* I told him. And, whenever possible, do no harm to animals or insects. Leave the wasps' nests, the bats, and the snakes. Yes, we've removed a few snakes from our yard, but we've transported them safely to an open field. Because I am bigger and stronger does not give me the right to crush everything in my path; it means I am responsible for smaller creatures. They do not seek me out to conquer my territory; I've encroached upon them, and if I handle them carefully and gently, they will not harm me.

As to answering his question about who made God, he would come to learn as he grows and matures that the mold for God could be found here on earth. God is a projection of our ideal selves: strong, invincible, all-knowing.

In the Beginning

In the beginning, when I "came out" to my kids, I was very worried about biasing them toward my views on religion. After all, I had come to my decision on my own as a young adult, and I wanted them to be free to accept or reject a God or gods and a religion, if they chose.

I tried—really hard—to be as objective as I could. I answered their questions with, "What do you think?" or "Let's look that up." I took them to church and listened to the preachers and priests. I talked to my kids about the Jewish, Islamic, Buddhist, Catholic, and Presbyterian faiths. I read Bible stories and took them to a Christian preschool and kindergarten. I told my kids about everyone's views but my own. Yet all along I felt the urge to tell them, "It's just a scam! God is no more real than leprechauns! Religion is big business!"

Then I realized that, little by little, I was letting myself in. I told them about the origins of God-kings and mythology and Christianity and the reasons why the Roman Catholic Church broke into so many parts. I was pointing out to them inconsistencies in religion and in the Bible, the "sameness" of stories across many faiths over thousands of years, and the discrepancies between what many folks say God should act like and the reality.

When we drove past a billboard in Clarendon, Texas, that read, "Jesus did not tap out. He loves you." I asked my kids, *Where? Where is Jesus if he did not tap out? How does he show us he loves us? How do I show you I love you?* I asked them. Try asking a kid those questions and see how quickly she understands the disconnect.

I asked my children why people pray if they believe that God gives everyone free will. If he is guiding us, righting our wrongs or affecting the outcome of a terrestrial situation, then we are not making our own decisions, are we? Why do some folks pray for God to help their football team win? You mean God cares about the Jets game and will fiddle with the football, but he doesn't care about the prayers of a nine-year-old who is beaten and locked in the closet? The scary thing is that a whopping 27 percent of *all* Americans believe that God affects the outcome of a sporting event, according to a 2013 poll conducted by the Public Religion Research Institute, and 53 percent of our citizens believe that God rewards faithful athletes with success and good health. Which begs the question: If God rewards the faithful, why are so many deeply religious countries also so poor? If people have poor health, does that mean they are not faithful enough? If God heals someone with cancer, why did he give that person cancer to begin with? It's not for us to know? Why not? This God we speak of is not very logical.

If you ask kids these questions, they will, no doubt, see the hypocrisy in the way we think about God and prayer. The words that come to mind are self-serving, selfish, shallow, and silly.

Now, with my kids awakened and listening to dialogue at school, among their peers, and on the news, I don't have to ask them anything. They know. And they are starting to ask and answer their own questions. While you've lost some sway as a parent when your kids start finding their own answers, that is one measure, albeit small, of parental victory.

What I Tell My
Kids about Heaven

This is my heaven. And, yes, sometimes, it is my hell and my purgatory. But I can think and love and move and eat and sing and smile. I can listen to the dry brown leaves scrape the pavement and watch the wind swirl them up into the air. I can look into the sky and see the sunlight stream through the clouds like tentacles, or I can watch the sun rise, a big orange fireball over the Atlantic. I can kiss the lips of a man and smell chocolate chip cookies baking. I can sleep and dream and hear the giggles of a three-year-old.

I can love my children's friends and my friends' children because they are my children, too. I can help my neighbor who is old and cranky but still cares about the world because I want him to keep feeling that way. In the summer, I can run through the rain and in the winter, I can throw snowballs. I can love the smell of fir trees and hate the smell of liver and onions.

I can write and think and let the words *I love you* roll off my lips and onto someone who will smile and say *I love you,* too. My memories can bring me comfort and make me smile. They can help me remember someone I once loved who has died. I can listen to songs and hum along or lie on the beach in the sticky salt air and listen to the cry of gulls. I can run fast and drive faster.

I can create myself with my thoughts, make stories with words, and paint images that move me. I can make love and make hate. I can feel the wind blow through my hair and feel the words of a loved one bite my heart with razor-sharp teeth. People can make me smile with their kindness, and they can make me cry with their cruelty.

My words can be a salve, a blanket, a thorn, a barb. I can throw my emotions at people—my anger and disappointment—and disable those I love, or I can speak softly, connect with kindness and encouragement, and build them up with positive thoughts.

This is my heaven, though sometimes it is my hell, too. This is what I know. All I know. The size and scope of this world and what I don't know is scary. It is much, much bigger than me. In the big picture, I am nothing. I do not exist. Yet this place, my presence in it, makes me feel alive. And even if my experiences don't always make me happy, I can still feel, I can still think, I can still breathe.

If earth is not our heaven, than what is it?

Creating a Moral Structure

osing your religion is like losing your virginity in two ways: You can never forget the moment you lost either one, and you can never get them back.

When I was a sophomore in college, my professor of American literature started to chisel away at our preconceived notions of faith. From the first day in that old stone building in North Carolina, with creaky wooden floors and high ceilings, he challenged our assumptions.

We began with the literature of the Puritans in colonial America. The austere and harsh religious views were a sharp contrast to the soft, feel-good religions that most of us students had experienced. The authoritarian focus on the Bible as law and moral edict are known today only to fundamentalists.

Next, we came to learn that the puritanical worldview would eventually shape American's confused perspective on womanhood and sex. The influence of the Protestant Christians, specifically the Puritans, probably added more fuel to the pornography fire than any other factor. (Well, save perhaps, for the Mormons.)

We moved on to the Age of Reason, with John Locke, Isaac Newton, and Ben Franklin. God was a giant clockmaker who set the world in motion and then left—or perhaps died. And the Devil? He faded away with the Calvinists' wrathful God. Then came Emerson, Thoreau, and transcendentalism, united by the belief that an innately good, unifying force pervades humanity and nature.

I was left alone: so many religious philosophies, so little time, but all unique and interesting. I realized that I could take apart my old Catholic views and reassemble a religion of my own.

One morning on my way to campus, however, my belief in God began to unravel. As I was driving to school, I heard on the radio about a boy who had been sodomized, tortured, and killed. It seemed as if I'd been hearing about that a lot lately. I imagined the child, reaching out to a trusting adult, only to be slowly and painfully murdered. I imagined the grief the parents felt, knowing that their son not only died, but horrifically so. It was not even my sorrow to bear, but I broke into tears. If there were an omnipotent God, he surely would not let this happen to an innocent child.

No explanation about God leaving us to our own devices could make sense of tortured children. No prayers that the faithful prayed asking God for silly things, such as houses or a new job, mattered. No one—and I mean no person, no matter how gifted in preaching—could convince me that a "kind and loving God" sits watching over us while allowing innocents to suffer. The God of the Bible—with all his supposed omniscience, power, and fatherly love—had failed as a parent. In an instant, I lost my faith. Those moments of clarity stick in your mind as long as you have memory. It was no different than the night I lost my faith in Santa Claus. Both quickly vanished as a real presence. Of course, my reasons for not believing, now, over twenty years later, are more varied and complex, fortified by years of thinking, reading, and reasoning with others.

There is a sense of loss and fear in the beginning: That gentle image of Jesus watching over us evaporates, erased from consciousness as a guide and a sentinel, now filed away as just another part of our world's flawed history. If there is no God, who will protect us and our loved ones? Bring us comfort? Calm our fears? Who are we without God? What is good? Who will judge us and mete out justice in the end?

You soon realize that there is also a great sense of freedom in losing one's religion, even as you realize that it is freedom from dogma that never made sense. You are suddenly master of your own fate and captain of your soul, to borrow words—a little out of context—from William Ernest Henley. You realize the enormous responsibility and exciting opportunity you have to re-create yourself, to craft the path you will take, to define the standards to which you will hold yourself accountable. You create the meaning in your life, your reason for living. This is also the gift we pass on to our children.

How do we define who we want to be, who we want our children to be? Just as a corporation has a statement of its values and mission, we have personal statements. They are usually kept in our heads. It's helpful to write out a statement of beliefs, and when your children are old enough, have them write theirs, too. What do you want to teach your children? What kind of men and women do you want to raise? Strong, independent, compassionate? Many traits will need to be tempered. For example, we want our children to be compassionate, but not so compassionate that they give all their savings away. How do we teach our children balance? Very early on I taught my children about money, savings, and investing, but I also made them give by volunteering either their time or their money. Of course, they will learn later that time is money, but you get the idea, and so did they.

Always encourage your kids to ask a lot of questions. Why should we share our time or our money? How much should we give? Do we have to? What are the benefits? What would happen to our town or nation if no one helped? If a friend asks you for money to buy lunch, but you don't have extra money, what should you do? Are there times when you should not share?

As our children grow and add new life experiences, their answers will change and grow more sophisticated. Questioning our children creates awareness, makes them feel that they are intelligent enough to find their own answers, and helps them become introspective, which is an important tool necessary in connecting their inner selves to their outside worlds. Kids who are introspective become adults who can understand themselves, who can communicate their thoughts, feelings, and the motives behind their actions. They will be able to express themselves and create healthy relationships this way.

Discipline without God

How do you discipline children after you take God out of the equation? One parent told me that, when he took his two kids to church, he expected the church to teach his son and daughter morals and discipline, especially when it came to sex. It's just easier to push these parental responsibilities off onto an institution that already has a structure in place to teach morality and discipline. The parent then becomes an agent of the church, reinforcing its teachings at home. But that is merely shrugging off our duties as parents by allowing religion to step in and indoctrinate our children.

There is no doubt that it is easier to team up with God, the guy many children have been taught to fear. God can see and do anything, including give eternal life and take it away. Yet these are just threats: An invisible deity is watching you, and if you're not "good," you will go to hell as a result. You will live in pain. Forever.

When we teach morals and discipline to our own children without religion, it takes a lot more effort, but we help our kids strengthen their own moral structure. Rather than telling children, "This is not how God expects you to behave," we tell them, "This is not how I expect you to behave—and you should expect more from yourself, too." As parents, we have to talk—a lot. We have to listen—a lot. We have to problem-solve and decide when to look the other way and let things slide, when to let things go with just a talk and when to impose some sort of punishment. It's not easy. If we are tired or stressed, our fuses may be short. I have yelled at my kids, only to have to turn around and apologize for raising my voice instead of speaking with calmness and control. I have made a lot of mistakes. None of us are perfect parents. What redeems us is that we love our children and are trying our best; when we let them down or fall short, we get back up and try to do better.

What is discipline? It's simply guiding children toward more appropriate behaviors. It has nothing to do with teaching or judging feelings—only actions. Unlike religion, we want to avoid personal attacks or judgments of character: Children are not dirty; they are not sinful; they were not born bad or evil.

Yet kids are born with certain tendencies, and their disposition has nothing to do with us as moms and dads. Some kids are easier to parent, and some are more difficult. Some understand the need for rules, while others see rules as a challenge, as a curb on their freedom. Keep on trying, knowing that your job as a parent means that you hang in there and encourage your kids to become the best they can be. Before you know it, they'll be eighteen and headed off on their own.

Hold tightly, but not too tightly. Have a lot of patience. Ask yourself: Would I want to be disciplined for that? Spilling a drink is no big deal. Spilling a drink after you asked your child not to bring it to his room is, obviously, a different issue. When we ask our kids to do something, give them a little time before they must "hop to it," but not so much time that they seem to have ignored us. Think of what it's like to be at work and have your boss ask you to do something, and then demand "Now!" Yet remember, too, that when your boss asks you to do something, you usually finish what you are doing and get started on the request. We have to teach kids to be internally motivated not just to do the right thing, but to do things at the right times.

Here are a few other suggestions:

- For young children (up to two years old), diversion and distraction are the best ways to redirect them. Lecturing or discipline at that age isn't very helpful.

- Point out the consequences of their actions. Hitting hurts me—see the red mark? Throwing balls inside the house breaks my favorite figurine from Aunt Helen.

- I don't believe in spanking, but I know some feel strongly that it is a good tool for children younger than ten, as long as it is not done out of anger and is only administered to the bottom.

- Avoid character attacks. (For example, "You're lazy.") Instead, offer reasons why cleaning up is important. "We have to keep our rooms neat so that we can find items when we need them." Or "We have to rinse and place our dishes in the dishwasher so that we don't invite bugs to live in our house."

- Give kids a little time on requests. "Please clean your room as soon as you are finished reading that chapter."

- Ask a lot of questions. "Why are you fighting with your sister? Is there a way to resolve this so you both can stop arguing and move on? How do you think arguing in the car is affecting the person who's driving?" If you treat children as if they are competent, they will learn that they are competent.

- When they are a little older—around age seven or eight, ask them to participate in discipline. "You disobeyed my request and could have hurt yourself or others. How do you think you should be disciplined?" Or "Your brother asked you not to take that toy from his room. Since you've broken it, what should you do to make amends?" Reparations can be made not just with money from their piggy banks, but also with their own toys or with work. ("I'll do his chores for a week.")

- When my son talked too much in school and the teacher notified me, I told him to write a letter of apology to the teacher, making sure that he noted why talking in class was not a good behavior. (It makes the teacher's job more difficult and distracts other students.) It's important to teach kids to respect authority at school and understand how their actions affect the group.

- Boys and girls have a lot of energy and are rambunctious, so when they start bouncing off the walls and knocking over lamps, tell them to run a couple of laps around the block. This is a great way for them to burn off energy and it helps them get into a better mood. Push-ups work, too, especially if you tell the kids that their old mom or dad can do more.

- Allow teens to help set some of their own boundaries. Tell them that you trust them to decide when they need to go to bed. A couple of late nights will help them understand that they need to care for themselves and get more sleep. For older teens, ask, "What time is a reasonable time to be home?" In our house, there are no curfews as long as certain conditions are met: My son tells me where he is going and when he will be back. And then he must be where he says he will be and be home when he has promised.

- Last, but perhaps most important: Punish sparingly. Instead, help kids recognize positive behaviors by acknowledging their kind words or helpful actions. If Johnny helps his younger sister get a toy from a shelf that she cannot reach, thank him for helping his sister. If your kids have an argument, and they are able to resolve their disagreement and move on, tell them how much you appreciate that they were able to work things out. Thank older kids for keeping their word, for helping pull their own weight, and for being a responsible part of the family.

If we put in the time to help kids learn how to regulate their behaviors and resolve conflicts early in life, as opposed to just imposing punishment for infractions, by the time they are teenagers, our job as parents will be much easier, and our children will make a smoother transition into adulthood.

Developing Critical Thinking Skills

I t doesn't matter if we teach our kids the alphabet before they get into preschool. They're going to learn their letters by the time they're five anyway. It doesn't matter if we teach them their colors. If they haven't picked those up through osmosis, they'll probably learn those, too, by the time they are five.

What kids really need to learn young is how to think—and how to have fun doing it. I'm not an expert in child development, but I did teach writing at a local college, along with a course called "Reading, Writing, and Critical Thinking." What I learned from my students was that many of them were not prepared to think critically or independently.

Why is this relevant to raising kids without religion? Because we are teaching our kids to reject dogma of all types, to question, to examine, and to process the information they receive every day. Teaching them how to think is one of the best gifts we can give.

Some of the same activities I used to teach my students, I also used at home with my own children. Of course, there is the usual suggestion to read. A lot. Read to them as long as they will let you. Let them read. Make them read. Tell them that it is a privilege to read over the summer. Many kids across the world don't have this luxury. Let them make their own books by stapling construction paper together and helping them write words. They can draw their own pictures or cut them out of magazines and paste them on the pages.

Here are a few other tips to help your kids all day, every day:

1. Teach your kids chess. It's known as the great equalizer because it's played by the old and young, rich and poor. No club membership or expensive equipment is required, and chess boards (for a cost of about $10) can travel everywhere you do. I'm a huge fan of the game (or sport, if you will). My father taught my brother and me to play when we were young, and I still remember how cool it was when I figured out how the horse moved. Chess helps develop critical thinking skills, strategy, concentration, and sportsmanship. When my kids were little more than two years old, I started teaching them the Pawn Game, a simplified version of chess. (See instructions on the next page.) Kids learn quickly. By the time mine were in elementary school, they were playing tournaments. I felt so strongly about the benefits of chess that I started a club at my sons' elementary school. It's easy to do. We even played tournaments against other schools that had chess clubs.

2. Television. Most parents these days limit television, and most of us even limit TV to watching public television. But kids do grow up, and somewhere around fourth or fifth grade my kids started asking me to watch the dreaded mainstream television programs—the "junk" stuff with commercials at which so many of us turn up our noses. Yes, eventually we all have to give in because children will hear about these shows from their friends at school, and they will watch them when they go to their friends'

THE PAWN GAME

Set up only the pawns—the game's "foot soldiers"—on the second row at each end of the board. The object of the Pawn Game is to be the first player to get one pawn to the last row on the opposite side of the board. On the first move only, a pawn can move directly forward one or two squares. After that, it can move forward only one square at a time. A pawn must move directly forward unless it is capturing another piece, in which case it can move one square forward on the diagonal. When the child understands how pawns can and cannot move, add a new piece to the board—a bishop, for example. For more information (and illustrations) see http://www.chesscorner. com/tutorial/basic/pawngame/pawngame.htm.

CHESS RESOURCES TO GET YOU STARTED

Chess Kids: www.chesskid.com
Chess Corner: www.chesscorner.com
The United States Chess Federation (USCF): www.uschess.org
(You'll also find resources here on how to start a chess club.)

homes or even download shows on their iPods. Withholding might simply make curious kids sneaky. Either we cede some ground or our kids will take it. So when my children started getting pretty persistent and telling me that I was depriving them of a normal childhood, I allowed them to watch "regular television" under one condition. They had to write at least one summary of a commercial during each thirty-minute program I allowed them to watch. (If you TIVO programs, don't fast-forward through the commercials.) Yes, they had to get out their pencils and papers and tell me what the advertisers were trying to sell and how they were trying to sell it. Were the advertisers trying to make us believe that everyone was buying a certain brand of juice, so we should, too? Were the advertisers trying to make us think that their product would bring us more happiness or make us more popular? You get the idea. I know you're probably thinking that, if you ask this of your kids, you'll be forever remembered as the world's meanest mommy or daddy. Not to worry—kids are very forgiving, and if you sit with them and watch (maybe with some snacks), they'll forgive you even sooner.

3. What's happening in this picture? I have several books with beautiful, glossy pictures. Some are famous paintings; some are photos of the world. These books do not have to be expensive. You can pick them up off the clearance tables at bookstores or check them out of the library. Let your kids pick the types of pictures and books they like. Then you can ask them questions like this, and they can respond verbally or in writing: What is happening in the picture (or photo)? What do you think happened before this photo was taken? What do you think happened afterwards? (You can ask them to imagine what happened before or after with paintings, too.) What was going on outside the painting? (For example, if the picture shows a couple on a busy street, what do you think was happening that you cannot see?) If there are people in the picture, do they look happy, sad, bored? Do you think the people are related? Why?

4. Read the paper together. You can do this in a variety of ways. During the summer, I asked my kids to find articles and write a short summary, giving me their thoughts on the topic as well as a recap of what the article was about. However, some kids are just suggestion-adverse. They have to do everything on their own time, at their own pace. My younger son used to sit at the table

in the morning and look over the headlines as he ate breakfast. Sometimes things would interest him enough that he'd read the whole article. I figured out that, if I just left the front page lying around, he'd look at it on his own, but if I asked him to look at something with me, of course he didn't want to.

5. Big boxes, little boxes, tins, sticks, old supplies—I had a big container of "stuff" that was no longer usable or that would eventually go to the recycle bin. I'd ask my kids, "What can you build out of all this stuff?" and we'd sit down and brainstorm for a bit. When they got busy, I'd sneak off and cook dinner. This is a great way to help kids think outside the proverbial box. I took pictures of some of the things they'd make: cars, houses, weapons, imaginary time machines. My kids would even pick up little things they'd find outside or discarded items in the stores (they'd have to ask first, before they took anything, even if it was a small clip). Everything became a potential building supply.

6. Teach your children to understand and recognize the difference between a statement of feeling and a judgment. This is important because sharing our feelings helps us convey honestly how we feel and can bring us closer to each other. When we judge, we present a statement as true or correct, and it makes us feel distant. Here are some examples. A judging statement sounds like this, "Religion is stupid." Or "You are dumb." A statement of feeling sounds like this, "I don't believe in God." Or "I don't like what you said about me."

7. Teach them to recognize stories and statistics that smack of big, fat exaggerations. The other day, a friend posted on Facebook, "Hammers kill more people each year than guns!!" (Gasp.)

Really? After a what-the-heck moment, I immediately went to FBI.gov, only to find that, "hammers, clubs, and other objects" kill more people than "shotguns," *but* the total number of deaths by guns of any type is greater. Far greater. In fact, "hammers, clubs, and other objects" are used in roughly 4 percent of murders, while a firearm of any type is used in nearly 68 percent of the murders in America. So let's teach our children to ask themselves, "Does that make sense?" Turn them into mini-researchers: "How can I verify this data?" Any website that ends in a .gov or an .org is usually more trustworthy than a .com. Teach them to check several references or resources and draw their own conclusions.

I Have a Plan for Me: How We Help Our Children Find Meaning

I took my kids to Red Mango one weekend (yum, yum), and there was a boy, around eight years old, wearing a black shirt with this written on the back: *God put me here for a reason and He has a perfect plan for me.* I don't know, but it just seemed that, if the T-shirt is true, then God is not a nice guy. I know there are kids born into this world who have terrible lives, who were just born into unfortunate situations—kids who die young of cancer, starvation, abuse. There are kids who are disfigured or caught in the middle of wars. Kids are born without homes or parents who love them.

Maybe I'm just getting old and grumpy, but it just seems that, if you really believe that God has chosen a special life for you, then you are failing to see the rest of the world. It's an egotism of sorts to think that God planned out your life when there are billons of people on this planet, many living in horrific conditions.

Maybe, like the Presbyterians, some folks think that their lives are a reflection of God's grace. I wonder if this boy's parents felt a sense of pride as they followed their chosen child out of the ice cream shop.

My kids are not so lucky. They have to make their own plans. Their directives won't come straight from above; they'll come in the form of a mere mortal (that would be me), questioning them about the world and how they can find their place in it. Their guidance in life will be the prosaic voice of a mother, telling them over and over again to do what they love, promote peace, and do the right thing.

One of the most important things I can teach them is that, while they are special to me, they are not special to the rest of the world. They are not deserving of or entitled to anything: They have to earn what they want, whether that is in school or in sports or in their first jobs. To the rest of the world they will be just another face in the crowd, another number, another kid who will slip unnoticed from high school into adulthood. It means they must have grit; they must have the determination to keep plugging away even when they face failures, even when they are tired and just want to rest. Being special is not about the gifts we inherit from the gene pool, it's about the determination and the passion and the drive we use to shape our futures. Grit is the great leveler.

To give their lives meaning, they will have to create it, since there is no point to living except for those reasons we assign to our lives. We are not needed to propagate the species: There are already plenty of us. In the end, we are all just along for the ride, no matter what we tell ourselves. Where we go, the stops we make, and the things we'll see—that's solely up to us.

I think I will print up a T-shirt for our kind of kids: *My parents gave me a life, and now I have to figure out what to do with it.*

New Commandments

Even if I believed that "the Lord came down upon Mount Sinai" and, for forty days and forty nights, issued a mere Ten Commandments to Moses, I'd still wonder why God hasn't come back to update his list. Who labors for six days and sits around all day on the Sabbath any more? Maybe this made sense generations ago when our grandparents farmed. Their work stretched out endlessly before them, and they were glad to take a day of rest at the end of the week. But now our days are a mix of work and play almost every day, including Sunday.

Some of the original commandments are oldies but goodies. They are worth keeping, but with updated language. So I thought the following would be a good start for a new list of commandments, though, no doubt this list could be even better. I've left a few blank lines at the end so you can add to it. The commandments should be a living list anyway, one that changes with the times, grows bigger—or smaller—as we grow as a people. Our commandments shouldn't be set in stone.

So what do commandments mean to those of us who don't believe there is a disciplinarian in the sky to whom we should bow? Our commandments are just a code to help us live peacefully and contentedly with others. We can say *goddamnit* without fearing heavenly retribution. We just shouldn't yell *goddamnit* at our neighbor when his weeds blow in our direction and seed our yard. We don't worry too much about offending someone because we work on Sundays, but we don't want to offend our coworkers with rude remarks or behavior.

Ask any nonbeliever, and he will most likely tell you that the most important decree to live by is the Golden Rule: Do unto others as you would have them do unto you. Though I was taught in Catholic catechism that Jesus Christ came up with these words, the Golden Rule is a thread that has run through most ancient cultures, thousands of years before Jesus was a baby bump in Mary's belly.

So here are the new commandments for modern life that we can teach our kids—by example, of course:

1. Do not hurt others or hurt yourself. The underpinning of treating others well is treating ourselves well, too, for we cannot give love and respect that we do not have. Do not hurt yourself with too much food or drink. Do not cause hurt through weapons or words or with irresponsible actions.

2. Do not lie, to yourself or others. Lying to yourself makes you an inconsistent, fragmented, and unhappy person. Lying to others decreases the value of language and increases our mistrust of humanity.

3. Don't take stuff that is not yours or that belongs to everyone. Stealing material goods obviously comes to mind, but we also steal other things. Businesses steal our clean resources when they pollute our air and our water. When we deface public property, we steal from others. If we have enough to eat, and we load

our plates with more, we take more than our fair share. The same goes for wasting water and other natural resources.

4. Talk respectfully, gently, and kindly to every person, especially those smaller or older than you.

5. Smile. Why include this simple, one-word commandment? Because life is so damn short that we owe it to ourselves, to our families, and to our fellow humans to be as happy as possible. We connect with a smile. A smile says, "I recognize that you exist and that you and I are here together."

6. Pick up trash that crosses your path. It's not someone else's responsibility to care for our mutual resources—it's yours and mine and our kids'. This planet was not given to us to "subdue"— it is only in our care because we are the most capable creatures alive. We've abused and used it because too many of us believe that we are the rulers and owners of every living thing on this planet. We are animals, too, albeit ones that have figured out how to remove our excrement from our homes and make shoes out of other animals. Humankind grew up here, grew greedy here, and we may become extinct here if we don't start ministering to our planet.

7. Care for animals that are injured and people who are hurt. When we extend a hand, we feel needed, and we feel good, but we also pass along a currency of goodwill, and that is crucial for all of us. Help others but, of course, don't be a crutch. Sometimes, the most important way to help is just by saying, "I'm here. I'm listening."

8. Don't hold on to hurt or anger or people you don't love or who don't love you. My Italian great-grandfather used to say, "Worry will kill you." So will hurt and anger that are buried. Nothing grows more malignant with age than bad feelings. Let go of experiences and people who have hurt you and live in peace.

9. _____

_____

10. _____

_____

What Is Good, and How Do We Teach Kids Right from Wrong?

Here's the problem with how the religious view us. A dad from Boston wrote, "A theistic worldview is the best grounding for why things like slavery, murder, and rape are wrong. Under an atheistic worldview, the universe is indifferent to the outcome of humanity, so why continue with the illusory notion of morality? Why continue saying that acts such as murder, rape, and slavery are right or wrong, good or bad when they are really just beneficial or not beneficial for the survival of humanity?"

On the surface, this dad was saying that morality, from an antitheistic worldview, is not necessary, that we would be free to do whatever we please. Yet, he also contradicts his own concern. Acts such as "slavery, murder, and rape" are "not beneficial for the survival of humanity," they are not considered good, and, therefore, regardless of whether one believes in God or not, are not encouraged. Because we are social creatures, society has its own moral strictures.

How do we teach kids right from wrong? Nonbelievers don't always do the right thing, but neither do believers. We can try to make choices that are beneficial, not just for us, but for others, too, because that's what gives our lives meaning and helps us all live peacefully. The majority of us—religious or not—seem to be hardwired for working together because we've evolved to realize that behaviors considered good or moral will help us secure a safe and stable place in our communities. Being "good" is not just good for us as a society, but also as individuals. Throughout history, humans who worked together were able to stay safe, obtain food, and reproduce. We have therefore evolved to work together, to sacrifice for our family, to have empathy for others who are suffering. We have evolved to understand that we are all contributing to the same Bank of Humanity.

You can see this morality in action in young children, albeit in more subtle forms. When my younger son had just started walking, I brought him to a meeting and tried to sit him on my lap. He was intent on watching a baby across the table. She was playing with a rattle in an infant carrier. When the baby dropped her toy on the floor and couldn't reach it, she started whimpering. The adults, of course, were busy. My son got off my lap and teetered around the table to give the toy back to the baby. I was surprised that he thought to do that at barely more than a year old. I did not teach him this behavior, and I try to remember, every time he talks back to me now as a teenager, that we—teenagers included—start off with good and caring intentions. The point is he was already becoming aware of others and learning that we all have to help out—I didn't even have to put the fear of God in him.

We are born not believing in anything. It's our natural state. There is no God in our brains until someone puts it there through suggestion, and the idea and the fear of God is no more likely to make people moral. Yes, going to church does teach good things, but for a price. It teaches kids to be good only because they will be rewarded with eternal life when it's all over. But this is a weak basis for morality because it focuses on doing what others say is right in exchange for an external carrot or reward, not on what each of us has reasoned is right. Even worse, you can do wrong over and over again, and many faiths offer forgiveness through a series of chants or prayers. Humans fail. Preachers fail. We are not all good, nor is it reasonable to try to make us pure, but we must be in control of our moral character and encouraged to grow.

As humans, we do have selfish impulses, yet being selfish is not necessarily bad. It's an impulse designed to keep and perpetuate life. Babies are incredibly self-centered and self-seeking because they have not learned to care for themselves. They have no consideration for others because they have not yet developed skills necessary to live. They cry for attention from Mom and Dad at all times of the day and night. As newborns, they impolitely turn their heads to search for a nipple when hungry, and when they get a few months older, they grab what they want without regard for others. Selfishness only becomes bad later in life if it supplants cooperation and compassion.

We are and will always be selfish in some way, even if it's just because doing right makes us feel good. And that's okay. But it's our actions, measured against society's standards, that make us good or bad. Our job is to teach our children, using their preprogrammed tendencies, how to choose behaviors that will help them and help their communities. Giving of one's time and one's self is the best way I know to teach these things. When my children were in preschool and elementary school, we delivered meals to homebound adults in our community through the Meals on Wheels program. Getting involved in community service early in life makes helping others seem like a natural part of everyone's routine. We teach kids to see that others need help, and since we're able, it's our duty to pitch in. You know what happens: What goes around comes back to you. Your kids, one day, will see you in your time of need and be compassionate. Raising kids to be kind and cooperative promotes peace.

I believe that our time is one of the best things we can give our kids to help them become good adults: Be present, listen, talk to them, tell them about your experiences, let them hear you talk to other people, have discussions, disagree respectfully, apologize when needed, say thank you, hug your family and your friends, smile a lot—not just to those you know, but to those you don't know. Hold yourself accountable for mistakes. Our kids learn from us, first and foremost. Teaching them moral behavior will help them function well in society and in all their relationships. This is how they learn how to be happy, too. Although we're not responsible for others' happiness, we do have a responsibility to be as happy as possible, not just for ourselves but for those around us. Yes, life is full of big hurts and small disappointments. Things you want and can't have and things you have but don't want. We have to train our minds to appreciate the things we have.

What Happens When We Die: Talking to Kids about Their Mortality

We used to have a tortoise, two dogs, two snakes, and various other little creatures we called pets. My older son, thinking he was doing a wonderful deed by letting his pet tortoise eat weeds under the swing set, learned an important lesson: Pets will, if they can, eat each other.

This happened one spring evening as I was working in the yard, the kids following me back to front to back and all around. We left the tortoise unchaperoned with two big dogs. Imagine how horrified I was, upon returning to the backyard, to find one of the dogs gnawing on something that looked like my son's pet tortoise. In fifteen minutes, the dog was licking out the inside of the shell as if he had just eaten tortoise soup. Why it seems funny now, I do not know, but when it happened I was horrified that my kids, trailing behind me like the tail of a kite, would see the carnage. So I immediately picked up the carcass and whipped it over the fence. My older son was immediately suspicious.

There's nothing like the death of a beloved family pet to jump-start conversations about death. Our dog, still licking her chops, was now a murderer. She would never lick one of us again as an innocent animal. Not only did I have to explain what happens when we die, I had to explain the whole animal instinct thing and why our dog ate our tortoise.

One of the most difficult aspects of raising kids without religion is teaching them about death. If I had a religion to rely on, I could tell my kids that, when they die, they will see a great light and be safely transported to heaven, where they will be greeted by God and every person who has ever loved them. Oh, and their pets. They'd see them again, too. They would then live a glorious life in eternity with all their friends and family and pets. They will feel no pain. They will want for nothing. (That actually sounds pretty boring, huh?) Just substitute the heaven narrative for rational thinking, and you don't have to face your fears. This is the easy way to deal with death—defer permanently the complicated and painful process of sorting through mortality. And you know what? I don't blame parents one bit for taking that path.

Of course, that's not the path I—and many others—chose. I'm comfortably certain there is no heaven and no afterlife, so I tell my kids as candidly as I can what *I think* will happen one day when they die. I have to tell them my truth, which will be their truth until they are old enough to decide for themselves. It is no secret that living without God and heaven does have its drawbacks. But it also has its benefits, including the ability to feel that you have majority control over your life, that you're not just a pawn under the capricious thumb of an imaginary person. I don't need to make things up when I don't have answers to questions such as: Where is heaven? What does it look like? How do we get there? As far as I know, this experience is the one shot we have, the only chance we will ever have to walk this planet and to have awareness.

It is easier the earlier you start—kids learn to accept death more readily when they are brought up thinking that it's an ordinary part of the life cycle. And, since they don't yet have a grasp of their own mortality, they don't get panicked over the idea that one day they will cease to exist. For moms and dads, especially those of us brought up believing in the afterlife, it's a different story. It's hard, very hard, to tell our children these things. Yet if you tell kids that this is the only heaven we know, that it does have suffering and eventual death, but you get the gift of life and so much potential for happiness in return, then they will learn to accept dying as a natural process and value the time they have sandwiched between birth and death. Like a roller-coaster ride, life has its ups and downs, its beginnings and endings and new riders. We are all taking our turns on this great ride. So much of our happiness hinges on these perceptions.

What I've told my kids about death is that their body is like a machine. When that machine is plugged in, it has energy; it has "life." When the cord is pulled, the machine is still there but it stops working. The body has "electricity" supplied by food, water, and good health, but when it no longer has these things, it stops working. The potential, the electricity it was once using, is rerouted to another source. Energy that comes from food will go to another organism. The body or shell left behind will become nourishment for plants, which will feed the animals. We will live on in the memories of those who knew us, at least for another generation or two.

When my kids were very young, they asked me to explain this concept several times. They were still grappling with the notion of death— even when they get to be my age, they will still be trying to wrap their minds around it. My kids seemed to feel OK with the idea that one day they'll be the flowers under a tree instead of thinking, breathing creatures. It makes them sad, they told me, but it's the circle of life. (Watching *The Lion King* helped.)

About our pet tortoise: My younger son, being a toddler, was oblivious to the fact that the tortoise was the dog's dinner, but my older son dealt with everything very matter-of-factly after the initial mortification.

He seemed to be on the verge of crying, but I honestly think he didn't break down because he was so curious about the dog's appetite. It was a new insight he'd just discovered.

I buried the pet tortoise in a Tupperware container at the end of our driveway while my kids were sleeping. The next day my older son asked what I did with the "body." I told him I made combs for my hair. Just kidding. I told him where the tortoise was buried. He wanted to see it, even though I explained to him that it might bother him or make him sad. It was not pretty.

But kids are remarkably resilient. I unearthed the shallow grave, and my son crouched down on his six-year-old legs and looked, emotion passing over his face. He was holding back tears. Then he stood up and told me he understood. It was the circle of life.

Crazy Kids
and Fearful Parents

As nonbelievers, we know there are no second chances and no alternate lives in another universe once this one ends. There is only this life, without a safety net. There is no such thing as miracles or fate, only luck and coincidences. I feel that this sometimes makes me hold tighter, figuratively and literally speaking, to my kids. This sense of motherly apprehension has been viewed by my younger son as shackles on his freedom.

The particular fear I have in mind is motocross racing. My son's father put him on a motorcycle at age four. He has been riding and racing ever since. And ever since I've implored him, I've begged and bribed him at every turn, to find another sport, one that was less dangerous and that offered him more college opportunities.

Yet some children are just born with a penchant for thrill seeking, along with the uncanny ability to pursue activities that will make Mom lose sleep. There is truth to the saying that kids give you gray hair. With every injury, I aged, if not visibly, then psychologically. It seemed that every time my son went out on the track, whether it was for practice or for a race, he was hurt. He's been in crashes, he's been crashed into, and he's had his bike land on his head and break his helmet.

Before you judge my parenting skills, let me jump in and give you a quick history. At age five, I took this matter to the law and asked them if there was any way to prevent my son from riding motorcycles at such a young age, but in the state of Texas—and perhaps everywhere—I learned that a child can ride at any age as long as he is properly equipped. I felt like a bad mom knowing that my kid was participating in such a danger- ous sport. When people would ask my children what sports they played, I cringed when my younger son would say, "motocross." After an uncom- fortable pause, they—strangers, friends, neighbors—would respond to him (while looking at me) that motorcycles are dangerous, *very* danger- ous. And I knew what they were thinking: You let your kid do *that*? What kind of mother lets her kid jump from cliffs, wrestle with alligators, and ride motorcycles? Then I would just smile and tell them that one of the biggest drawbacks to divorce is that you get absolutely no say at the other parent's house.

After nearly a decade of living in fear that I would bury my son before he buries me, I finally talked myself into a different understand- ing of his choices and behaviors. My son's passion for racing motorcycles keeps him focused in school—it's the only thing he cares enough about to hold out as a bribe. He lifts weights so that his legs and arms will be stronger for riding. He eats a healthy diet, forgoing candy, so that he can be a healthier athlete. Some people live their entire lives and never find something they feel passionate enough about to give up candy. Isn't that what we tell our kids—do what you love?

He has worked so hard doing what he loves that at age fourteen, he already has sponsors. And what I've come to realize is this: If he is successful, if he arrives mostly intact, at the end of his motocross days, then he will have confidence that no money can buy, that no mother could give. He will learn that there is a correlation between effort and success.

He will learn that grit and passion made him one of the best. If I keep him from doing what he loves, from what he tells me he lives for, I will crush his dreams and kill his passion. I will emotionally knock him down and teach him that my fears can circumscribe his life at any point and take him hostage. I would take from him the thrill that his personality craves for a sport, an adventure.

I'm still painfully aware that my son could end his life while riding a motorcycle, but the alternative of not riding seems just as painful for him. If the life we give our children in creating them is a gift, then I cannot add conditions to it. Gifts are given freely with no strings attached.

Who Needs Church?:
Keeping Kids Out of Trouble

Some people think that church involvement keeps kids out of trouble. That may certainly be true, but I've also seen a lot of cases where involvement in church has had no effect. Around here, a lot of parents drop their kids at Young Life, a Christian youth organization, so that they can have a worry-free night off. Yet you hear all sorts of stories that make you realize parents shouldn't be checking their worries at the church door.

There are no guarantees any of us can keep our kids "out of trouble." What do I mean by staying out of trouble? I mean staying away from alcohol and drugs, making it through childhood without having children of their own, staying out of the legal system, being successful in school, and moving on to college or trade school after graduation.

A few things will help. Of course, parental involvement tops the list. That means not just being there for your kid physically, but being there emotionally, ready to listen and problem-solve, not shame and blame. This is something I've had to learn and relearn, especially when I'd get caught up in my own work, grading papers or writing. I have to remind myself that my kids don't just need my physical presence. They need me actively engaged, even if we're just driving in the car to tennis practice. Talk. Ask lots of questions. Have the sleepovers and the get-togethers at your house so you can get to know your kid's friends. By getting to know his friends, you'll know your kid better, too. You'll know where he is and what he is doing. I know it's a pain in the ass to be the host all the time, to provide the food and to have a constant stream of noise and activity, but one day, he'll be grown and on his own, and you'll have plenty of quiet time on your hands.

One high school student from Virginia, Ryan, identifies himself as agnostic. He used to go to church with his grandparents when he was younger because his parents, both agnostics, wanted to give him a taste of religion. He felt it was a waste of time and thought it was silly to sing about "a big man up in the sky." When he had to go to church with his grandparents, the kids were often separated from the adults and taken to another building. Ryan said he hated being stuck with a group of "clique-ish" boys he couldn't relate to.

Ryan's mom no longer makes him attend church with his grandparents, and he enjoys spending time with his parents and two sisters instead. He told me, "We do a lot of things as a family. We all go out and play tennis, and we do a lot of activities outdoors, like camping. One small thing we do every night is eat dinner together and talk about controversial issues, which my mom researches and we discuss. We also watch television together once a week. None of us really has the time to watch TV, so my parents tape one interesting program a season, and we sit down and watch it together."

For younger kids, some ideas for entertainment at your house can come in the form of toys, movies, board games, cupcake decorating, mov-iemaking, water balloon fights, and Slip 'n' Slides. For the older kids, set up a volleyball or badminton net, a basketball goal, a croquet game. The big kids love water balloon fights, too, and board games like Headbands or Pictionary (try Craigslist or eBay for any of these items if they are too expensive to buy new).

Carrie is raising her three kids without religion. She shares this: "I'm about raising compassionate, involved, loving children. And so far, without religion, it's going great. They don't have to waste three hours every Sunday fighting boredom like their friends who attend The Church of Jesus Christ of Latter-Day Saints (and then several other hours during the week for various church-related activities). They don't have to reject people because someone tells them a book says so. They're free in so many ways that I wasn't at their ages. In this family, it's working really well."

Another mother, who used to be a Jehovah's Witness, said that her family has more time for "various charities and community efforts. It's much more satisfying than the 'preaching work.' I see direct results of my efforts and feel a sense of accomplishment. There is more time to spend together as a family, just talking. Jehovah's Witnesses are told that attending meetings as a family is 'quality time.' It's not. Anyone with children knows that sitting mutely listening to Bible lectures for two hours straight is not 'quality time' spent with your children."

Other families spend their Sunday mornings cooking breakfast together. "We have fun making up different types of pancakes," one mom said. "We also spend at least one night a week hiking the trails near our neighborhood, going bowling, or riding bikes. We try to be active together at least one night a weekend; more if we can."

There are other ways to help our kids stay out of trouble and stay focused in school. Starting around age five, I told my kids that they had to choose one sport to play and one instrument. They could choose anything they liked, and they could switch at any time, but they had to do one of each.

Playing an instrument is like learning another language; it helps our kids' brains grow and become more flexible. Try a Google search and you'll find many studies that support these claims and more. Children should be encouraged to try out several instruments, and then, as they grow, to pick their favorite. Reading music and mastering a few songs gives kids a sense of accomplishment and teaches them discipline. The time they spend taking lessons and practicing is less time they have sitting around, but I'm not going to sugarcoat this. When your little maestro starts out, you'll probably want to invest in a pair of earplugs or set up a practice area in a remote corner of your home. Yes, it's that bad. I realize that instruments can be expensive, too; again, you can often find good deals on eBay or Craigslist. Ask friends if they can recommend a music teacher. You can also find free lessons online through videos.

Sports are important because they teach kids to care for their bodies and to value what their bodies can do. Studies have shown that kids who play sports are less likely to use recreational drugs, less likely to grow into obese adults, and more likely to do well in school. The increase of blood flow helps move more oxygen and other nutrients to the brain, which has all sorts of cognitive benefits.

The key thing is that parents not become invested in their child's wins or losses. Playing sports should be fun and driven by the child's motivations. There's enough pressure on kids without having to worry about disappointing Mom or Dad if they lose.

As my kids grew older, I told them to pick the sport they love most, one that gave them the most enjoyment to play. I wanted my kids to learn to follow their passions. My older son picked tennis, and, as you read in a previous essay, my younger son picked motocross. They weren't my choices—as I mentioned, I definitely would have picked a less dangerous sport than motocross—so it gives them a sense of ownership over their decisions and their participation. As they grow and master their chosen sport, they will understand that it's solely their investment to make, and that it does have returns. But in the meantime, practicing, playing, stringing racquets, or repairing motorcycles—all of these activities are learning opportunities that will help keep kids busy and on a path that will have future payoffs.

Guardian Angels:
What I've Taken from My Children

This sounds strange, but maybe another mother has had these thoughts, too.

Do you ever worry about your children growing old, about them growing old alone with no one to love them? These thoughts really distress me. I think of my kids as elderly and fragile, walking through a quiet, dark house with no one to love them or to look out for them. I think of them lying in bed and being afraid. I don't want them to be afraid. Or alone.

When I was a kid growing up Catholic, I used to keep a glow-in-the-dark rosary under my pillow. When I was scared of the dark or upset about something, I'd reach under my pillow and hold the rosary in the dark. It made me feel safe. It made me feel connected to a strong, all-knowing, wise being who loved me no matter what I did or thought. I've never told anyone about this before because it all sounds so silly. I really felt as if a higher power were watching out for me, though I know now that it's unrealistic—and narcissistic—to think that I had a special angel who followed me everywhere, even to the toilet. Yet it's what adults had told me; I had a guardian angel and somehow that gave me a sense of security.

There are good reasons for not indoctrinating my kids into a religion, but this is what I have taken from them: Feeling comforted in the middle of the night by belief in a supreme being and guardian angels, even if they are not real, because the power of believing trumps reality.

How do our children find comfort instead? When they are young, they have you to give them comfort. If you want them to feel that they are part of a "spiritual" but not religious community, I recommend Buddhism or the Universal Unitarian Church—and now there are even a handful of atheist churches. As they get older, kids can learn to calm themselves through meditation or through a connection with a friend or sibling. They can exercise, which is calming and releases endorphins, or lose themselves in a good movie or a good read.

Children need to know that they can find comfort within themselves and around them: Let them know that, ironically, we are all united by our loneliness, by the solipsism we feel at night when we turn off the lights. These are normal feelings that others understand. Accepting these worries that occasionally surface is the small price we must pay for the exquisite opportunity to walk this planet, to experience love, and to have breath.

Why Moms Pray

The kids are on a trip with the grandparents. Wa-hoo, you might think. Sleep late. Watch TV. Eat junk food.

But for me, it brings sadness. Every time my children leave, it is another cut in the parental umbilical cord. It's the sad process of letting go, of realizing that, while they slip away from me and become independent adults, I will still worry about them. The mothering cord is never cut.

My kids flew out to Yellowstone for a grandparents/grandchildren adventure. They will create memories for five days, saving a few salient ones to take with them through their lives until their memories fail. It was a wonderful opportunity for them, and on the surface I was happy that they had the opportunity.

But I awoke at 2:30 a.m. in a panic and stayed awake for the rest of the night, worrying futilely about things I had no control over anyway: the safety of my kids' travels, how they would behave, and if they would be homesick.

I thought for a fleeting moment about praying, and I understand why so many mothers have prayed for their children in the long, dark night. There is no salve for the sick feeling that your babies are at the mercy of nature and society. There is no cure for the heartache of watching something you created and loved so intensely take flight and fly away from the safety of your nurturing care.

Children outgrow us so fast. They leave us behind holding only memories of their life with us.

So, even though I don't believe in God, don't believe in an afterlife, when I hear another mother say that she prays for her child, I know how she feels.

Prayer, Clarity,
and Self-Comfort

I need prayer. We need prayer. Not in the way you might think, though.

Traditionally, the act of praying asks another "person," a god figure, for things (stuff, strength, comfort, decisions) we should be asking from ourselves. People also pray for clarity: *God help me decide, help me find my way.* Yet you and I know that either we make our own decisions or decisions are made for us through our lack of action or through poor choices (as in the case of breaking the law, when the court system may decide our future for us). Though it would sometimes be nice, we cannot abdicate our responsibility for decision making to an imaginary person. We have to sift through choices ourselves, and it's often difficult.

For me, at least, it's really difficult. Like many of us, my mind sometimes feels like a hornet's nest that's been knocked down, or like a busy highway that doesn't have speed limits or signs telling me where to go. When the world becomes complicated and hectic, it becomes hard to focus, hard to concentrate, hard to organize. I think most of us are like this: We have really busy, chaotic brains.

That's where meditation comes in. (Note that I said meditation not medication—the difference one little letter makes!) It's been practiced by many different religions since the beginning of time. Both prayer and meditation are similar in that they direct awareness inward, away from the business, and busyness, outside our brains and bodies.

Meditation is extremely relaxing. Though some people claim it helps them regulate their internal body processes or gives them superhuman benefits, for me, it's sort of like taking a broom and sweeping out all the dust bunnies and dog hairs. It helps me concentrate, focus. It helps me be still. It even helps me fall asleep.

The very first time I tried to meditate, I was in my early twenties and severely stressed. I tried to use it as a way to avert migraines and calm my fears. Meditating is one of those things you have to try a bucket-load of times before you understand why it's good. You have to train your mind to be still, to reach flow. This is a process.

As a parent, meditation is a great way to deal with stress, but it is also a good habit to teach our kids, whether directly or just by example. Some researchers say that meditating helps increase intelligence and academic performance and that it was pivotal in early humans' development of attention and working memory.[1] But the value in meditation is the ability to comfort oneself. You and your kids can use meditation as others would prayer—to deal with stress, anxiety, illness, fear.

There are many ways and types of meditation. Tracy Carruth, E-RYT 500, AYS, is owner of Yoga Balance Studio, a registered yoga school.[2] She shares a simple method of meditation for nonreligious parents:

---

[1] Matt J. Rossano, "Did Meditating Make Us Human?" *Cambridge Archaeological Journal* 17 (2007): 47–58. For more published research on the benefits of meditation, visit http://www.tmbusiness.org/tm-research/references.html.

[2] One of the highest yoga certifications, *E-RYT 500* stands for Experienced Registered Yoga Teacher, 500 hours training. *AYS* is an acronym for Ayurvedic Yoga Specialist.

There are many techniques for meditation—it is beneficial to explore different practices to find one that resonates with you. One meditation practice I find helpful is to simply rest in silence. There is no goal, nothing to do, nothing to accomplish, nothing to improve upon. Methods aimed at achieving a certain state of mind can lead to grasping and dependency, which move you away from the intent of the practice—to abide in awareness.

When thought is not being manipulated or controlled, consciousness spontaneously appears. When you first begin to meditate, thoughts, emotions, images, sounds, body sensations, and memories arise. We have been conditioned to judge, analyze, label, and create stories around these objects of our mind. As the mind attempts to control that of which it is aware, it begins to make assumptions based on past conditioning and habitual patterns.

In this particular practice, all constructs of the mind (thoughts, feelings, emotions, memories) are left to their natural functioning. This means that no effort is made to focus on, manipulate, control, or suppress any object of awareness. In this meditation practice the emphasis is on residing in pure awareness itself—not on being aware of objects. This is the space in which all objects arise and fall away.

As you gently relax into awareness, the mind's compulsive thinking around objects will soften and fade. Complete relaxation and awareness in the silence of being will bring you into greater consciousness. An attitude of being receptive and nonattached will support the presence of silence and stillness, qualities of our true nature.

As you rest more deeply into the comfort of stillness, your mind releases compulsion, identification, and judgment to allow for space beyond all knowing; clear awareness returns.

Should you become ensnared in the mind's activity, you can use a more directed technique. Following the breath or using a simple mantra or repeated phrase may help prevent you from getting lost in thought. At some point, let go of the technique or return to simple observance as meditator, and gently rest in silence.

If fear or painful memories arise—do not resist, indulge, or analyze. Alternatively, allow them to rise and fall away without resistance. You can ground yourself by anchoring your attention gently on the breath. Resisting often increases difficult emotions, so remain unmoved by the body or mind's illusion, and continue to ground yourself with positive intention and breath. Likewise, this technique of passive observance is helpful when the mind is distracted by various images, ideas, and other stimuli.

If you receive a sudden insight, quietly receive it with gratitude, allowing it to move with equanimity and trust that it will be there when you need it.

If you need more guidance, check out a local yoga studio, meditation meet-up, or classes at a community college. For information online, visit the website of the National Institutes of Health's National Center for Complementary and Alternative Medicine, http://nccam.nih.gov/health/meditation.

Old Moms

So my younger son says to me one day, "I wish you had me when you were younger." And I tell him that thirty-three (the age that Jesus died) was not *that* old, and that older parents are usually more patient and "settled." And he says, "But I get to spend less time with you before you die. Some of my friends have known their parents since they were twenty-two." I assured him he'd still have plenty of time to spend with me (Hell, he'll get tired of me by the time he turns eighteen) and that he should also wait until he's older than twenty-two to have kids. (Couldn't resist.)

I told him that I'm taking care of myself so I can still be a young old person. I pointed out that I don't do drugs, smoke cigarettes, or go squirrel-suit flying, even though, as an adult, I can do these things if I want. Instead, I choose what I eat and drink carefully, wear a helmet when skiing and biking, and exercise my body because it was meant to be moved. Although it's true that I'm a certain age, there are things I have control over—and he does, too.

What he said, though, about having less time to spend with me, made me smile, and I savored it for a bit. I thought about my older son, who is on the road to independence and no longer cares if he has parents. Soon, my younger son will cut the cord emotionally, too.

I wondered if having doubts about an afterlife has made him even more aware of how finite our time is together. This is one of the times I wished I could tell my kid not to worry. We'd all be together one day in heaven. Actually, it was one of those times that I wished I believed that.

Sex, Sluts, and Madonnas

Religion tends to spoil sex. Christianity, in particular, always has. It teaches guilt. It teaches abstinence. It drives desire underground, but it does not go away.

When I was growing up, good girls didn't do "bad" things like have sex, smoke, and salute with their middle fingers. They didn't initiate sex, they didn't want sex, and they felt bad after getting it. Good girls said no. If a girl *did* want it, she was cheap. If a boy wanted it, he was just being a boy.

Where did all these sexually blasphemous ideas come from? If my college professor was to be believed, it was the Puritans. Women were supposed to be pure and chaste. Sexual desire was sinful. Yet even before the Puritans, Christianity held the view that sex was evil and that woman was innately morally depraved and the source of temptation. Woman was the reason for original sin. Ironically, we can thank Eve for being both the source of our fall and the reason we are here. For thousands of years we've carried the idea that woman = sex = sin.

At some point, though, we came to view intercourse and virginity as the gift women would "give" their husbands on their wedding night.

A woman's worth was determined by her hymen. Later, advertising brought sex into the public eye, and the vixen was born. She was every man's dream—sexy, compliant, and full of desire. She was not ashamed to admit that she wanted it. Her libido was more evenly matched with the male libido. Men, who've had the luxury all along of expressing lust, never had to hide their desire.

This duality caused females to fracture into two types: those who openly admit they want sex (whores) and those who want it but won't say it (Madonnas). We do a huge disservice to our girls and boys with all this purity BS. Women are either unspoiled or spoiled goods. There's no in-between.

You would think we've come a long way, but, truly, we haven't. I still hear teenage girls talk about the "sluts" who flirt with their guys. Ever heard a guy call a fellow male a "whore" for checking out his chick? Don't think so. Boys don't have to worry about these labels. Their market value is not determined by their coital history. Even teens realize that only females are defined by their sexuality.

This double standard in relation to sex causes a lot of dysfunction in relationships and marriages. And it's not fair to our girls. We should celebrate that we are all sexual beings, able to connect both physically and emotionally. Women are not supposed to be Madonnas. Nor whores. They are supposed to enjoy sex just as much as their male counterparts—and we should take the guilt out of sex so that our daughters can have healthy relationships with their own bodies and with others.

I'm not suggesting that women rut like rabbits or that we give a thumbs-up to our girls when they want to bed their first beau. Boys and girls should both be taught from birth to treat their bodies as temples to be respected. Just as they must wait to drive and to vote, there should be a certain age where sex becomes suitable. (Not fourteen years old.) Our children need to be emotionally ready, too.

I've tried to impress on my kids the emotional and physical risks associated with sex. You have choices, I've told them; you have to be discriminating. Every time you have sex, you give away part of yourself. If you give away too much, eventually you will have no self-respect left. You should know why you want to be intimate. In life, you will have reasons for choosing a career, a job, a house, and friends; don't just choose someone to have sex with because she's a warm body or because you can. You *can* take drugs; you *can* eat too much. You should be able to list the reasons why you love a person. You have standards for the decisions you make in your life, and you should have standards for the person you decide to bed. Make sure you are ready. You can never go back. In that one act, you are entrusting your emotional and physical well-being to another, and there is always the possibility that your decision can lead to a lifetime commitment in raising a child or a lifetime struggle with a sexually transmitted disease.

Girls: Subjects and Objects

There is a lot of pressure for girls to date and find boyfriends in high school. Laura, an agnostic mom from Florida, is raising a daughter. She explains her approach to teaching her teenager about gender roles and self-image:

> I told my daughter that, in language, there are subjects and objects. The subject is what is doing the action, and the object is what is receiving the action. In life, men have historically acted as subjects and women as objects. A lot of women present themselves as objects: They dress in a certain sexually revealing way and act flirtatious to attract men.

> I point to examples and tell her, "That is what you would look like if you were going to be an object. I am raising you to be a subject so that you can be a scientist or a lawyer, not the wife of a scientist or the wife of a lawyer. Professional women in top positions don't dress and act like that. Think about

*yourself, see yourself, and project yourself as a subject. If you
present yourself as an object, men will treat you like one, but
if you present yourself as a subject, men will treat you as an
equal, as a subject instead.*

*"Be pretty in a natural way by using your personal charms
rather than your sexual charms. Don't be in a hurry to
find a boyfriend. Pursue your own interests. Develop your
friendships. Don't feel pressure to be like the girl down the
street who has already had seven boyfriends by the ninth
grade. Look for the boys who tend to be more on the quiet
side, the boys who are less showy, the ones who aren't racking
up the girlfriends throughout high school. Teens who wait
to date later on are usually the ones who will have stronger
relationships when they do find someone they like."*

■

ERIC'S STORY: A DAD'S PERSPECTIVE

As parents, we know our kids are going to learn about sex from their friends
at school, from the media, and from their smartphones. So, we can either let
them absorb whatever they can from wherever they can, or we can inform
them ourselves and teach them the things we believe will protect them.

Many of us have learned from our parents what not to do. This was
the sex talk Eric, an agnostic father from Atlanta, received when he was
a teenager. He writes:

*When I was a teen, my mother loaded my sister and me in the car and
drove us around the block.*
Mom said, "Please. Promise me that you will not have sex."
"OK. I won't," I said. (Same response from my sister.)

"Promise me?" she responded.

"I promise, Mom!" was my final answer.

"Now, promise me you won't take drugs." This was my mother's educated approach to drugs and sex.

"I promise not to take drugs, Mom."

We got out of the car and went back inside. All done—the subject was never discussed again. Needless to say I had already smoked weed (if you use the term pot with your children it makes you appear unknowledgeable) and had already been drinking for a while.

Eric is now raising a young daughter and a teenage son. He did not want that to be the extent of the talk with his kids. He shares his experiences with teaching his son the responsibilities of growing up and of becoming sexually active:

There's so much to discuss with our children about sex. It's not an easy thing, but it has to be done. If you talk with them, they usually, in turn, talk to you.

He tells of two experiences that shaped his and his wife's views as parents teaching their children about sex:

My wife's mother's approach to her daughter was rooted in the Southern Baptist realm of ideals and was what I believe to be a scare tactic from religion. "If you have sex prior to marriage your husband will know. A virgin bleeds. It is against God to not be pure for your husband." Now, my wife did not want to live her life in small-town South Georgia. She had plans to "get the hell out of dodge" and never look back. That is what she did, and it was based on her drive and willingness to work hard and put herself first before ever thinking about sex and/or marriage. If she didn't focus hard and follow her path, she may have ended up staying in South Georgia. My wife was never offended by her mother's words. She realized, as I did, that this was an approach to sex akin to my own mother's, making me promise to never take drugs or have sex. (OK, Mom, I PROMISE.)

My sister had the same talk as I did, and yes, she answered the same way: I promise, Mom. I won't do drugs and have sex. Luckily, my sister turned to her best friend's mother to have a real conversation about growing up and becoming a teenager/adolescent. One of her reasons for turning to somebody else partially stems from the following incident. My mother's second husband was a physically, verbally, and sexually abusive alcoholic. I never experienced anything sexual from him, but my sister did. He felt that it was okay to touch her inappropriately. My sister went to our mom and told her. Her response to her ten-year-old daughter was, "Stop being promiscuous!" End of conversation. Five years later she was asking her daughter to promise not to have sex. Not my approach with my own children.

In neither of these experiences were these two girls taught about love in a relationship, STDs, what a boy thinks with, and the strength of the word NO. They didn't teach about morality. They only taught, "Just don't do it."

Well, I have a sixteen-year-old son. What can I do to teach him about the morality of sex? I never knew how I would do it, and, trust me, it comes out a bit fragmented, but we do discuss these issues. We talk, and I try to be as straightforward with him as possible. Our most recent discussion was on the topic of buying condoms. My son will be a senior and he just started going out with his first girlfriend. He has his license and a job. We've had conversations about sex, drugs (for us a big conversation about marijuana), and teenage parties. We continue these talks regularly. There is a lot of responsibility that comes with becoming a teenager, and sometimes teens need help figuring out their responsibilities.

So who buys the condoms? Do I buy condoms for my son? No, I do not buy him condoms. It would be really weird for me to buy condoms for him. It's his responsibility. So, I sometimes need to reiterate what we have talked about in regard to condoms, women, and STDs. First, son, always respect a woman. I cannot stress this enough. If a woman says, "No," then it is NO. If you think your sexual urge is too strong, go masturbate.

Second, remember that sex is a very intimate act between two people. Learning about being in relationships is much more valuable than just wanting to have sex. You have to remember that the majority of folks will be in multiple relationships in high school, college, and afterwards. When the time is right for you and your partner, you both should be properly prepared. So, son, you need to go out and buy condoms. This does not mean that I am giving you permission to have sex. I am telling you that you need to be properly prepared. I never had sex until I was in college, but I did buy condoms. I would have to go buy more if the ones I bought expired. You will have to do the same. And, please remember that condoms do not protect against all STDs and cannot be 100 percent effective against any STD or getting a woman pregnant.

As Eric shows, neither parents nor teenagers feel comfortable having the sex talk. But it is easier if you start a dialogue when your children are very young (when they begin school) and periodically revisit the topic. While books are helpful to supplement your talks, they are no substitute for your advice and guidance.

There is a misconception that Godless = valueless, but you and I know that there is no correlation between religion and morality. The important thing we want to convey to our children is that sex does not happen the way it's portrayed in the movies—rather, it's a serious consideration that carries a lot of emotional and physical risks and responsibilities. It is a beautiful thing when it's part of a committed relationship, and waiting for the right partner and being conscientious not only shows that they value the person they're with, but also that they value themselves.

Terrorists

O h, e-mail, the modern form of communication that gives people a way to be meaner, and faster, anonymously.

I received another one of those e-mails that has been forwarded about five thousand times. This one asked me to boycott Walmart because the company supports gay rights. The vehemence of some folks' disapproval would make you think the stores were selling child pornography. The message said that Walmart had overstepped "His boundary" by promoting the homosexual agenda, and now Mr. Walton was going to suffer the consequences of losing his good, God-fearing, Christian customers who are beyond reproach on all things and who follow the loving example of Jesus Christ. These Christians were going to start shopping at "local stores" instead.

So I immediately go to my children and tell them about homosexuality, why adults should have the right to choose who they love, and why it's none of our business what other consenting adults do as long as they don't harm anyone. They are young enough that they still listen to me, still trust that what I'm saying is The Word. I could just as easily teach them hate as I could tolerance. I top off our talk with a recap about healthy relationships, whether heterosexual or homosexual.

I actually considered *shopping* at Walmart after reading the e-mail, but I seriously doubt the soldiers of Christ sending the hysterical call to arms will pass up the cheap deals at America's preferred big-box store in favor of helping the "local" guy and gal. That would mean money out of their pockets. When weighing pocketbooks and principles, the wallet always wins.

What's disturbing, however, is that these religious hound dogs try to incite frenzy over ideas they "don't believe God honors." How would they know? Does God talk to Walmart shoppers? If this is a belief—and a very personal one at that—then why bully others into following it? Isn't this intimidation a form of terrorism?

Note to my children: If you know people who participate in these types of boycotts, avoid them.

Can Two Boys Marry?

My son once asked me this question, "Can two boys can marry?" *No,* I told him, *not in Texas and not in most states.* He was okay with my answer. I asked him why he asked this, thinking a teacher or a student had said something at school.

"No reason," he said. "Just wondering." I took the opportunity to help him think this out.

Do you think two men should be allowed to marry, I asked?

"I don't know." Of course, that is a typical ten-year-old answer. Kids don't normally have strong opinions at that age unless they've been spoon-fed an adult's views. They take everything with a proverbial grain of salt. I can see how easy it would be to program my kid—any kid—with an emotion-laden response, a response such as, *Men who love other men should have their arms and legs torn off and will be left to burn in hell for all eternity.*

Would it hurt you or me if two men married? I asked him.

"No," he said. *Then do you think we should tell other people how to live their lives if they're not hurting anyone?*

"Of course not," he said.

That's what I think, too, I told him calmly. *Just because people are different doesn't mean they shouldn't have the same rights.*

There are enough serious issues in the world for people to get behind: hunger, cancer, climate change, child prostitution, and human rights abuses. There are fifty more issues that I can rattle off to rally behind. Gay marriage really isn't a threat to anyone, except for the businesses that would have to offer benefits to spouses. We shouldn't be wasting time and energy fighting over what two men or two women do in their personal lives.

■

ANNA'S STORY: THE HURTFUL EFFECT OF RELIGIOUS IDEOLOGY

Anna is a fellow blogger, the mother of a toddler, and a nonbeliever. She shares her moving experience of how losing her faith set her free, but also how hurtful religious ideology can be:

My father was a jailhouse convert. That's what they call people who "found the Lord" in jail. He went to jail for drug possession, possession of marijuana paraphernalia, and attempt to distribute. I was fifteen when he went to jail and I was among the people praying for his salvation. When he was released, I had a new and improved "Christian Dad." He went from dealing pot to dealing Bible verses; instead of handing out $20 bills, he was dealing out prayers.

I was a crusader for the Lord and excited to know my prayers were answered; I quickly learned that my prayers backfired. At first it was little things; he did not speak to me for six months after I dyed my hair when I was sixteen, because my body was a temple and I shouldn't alter the way

God made me. He "disowned" me for another few months when he found out I was having premarital sex with my boyfriend. It was a quiet sort of condemnation, but nothing we couldn't always come back from.

While at college, after a long string of events, I woke up one morning and thought "I think I'm gay." It's surreal, even now, thinking how quickly I washed the men right out of my life and embraced this new identity. However, this identity came with a bitter aftertaste. Could I still be a crusader for the Lord if I loved another woman? When I came out to my father, he gave me my answer: NO. I could not love God and love another woman.

He told me I made a deal with the Devil, and I was going to hell. The moment I came out I became a stranger to him, someone he couldn't know. He was told by the church authority that if he allowed me or my partner into his home, I would corrupt his other children and condemn the entire family to hell with me. He would send me long-winded letters about how scared he was for my salvation and begged me to turn from my "wicked" ways. I spent the first six years of my relationship with my partner in tears—and in fear for my soul.

It took longer to wash God out of my life. I was in constant fear that my dad and the church were right. I developed an anxiety disorder built on the fear that if I died, where would I go? What would happen to me? The fear tactics of the church took a heavy toll on my life and, over time, on my relationship. My partner stuck by me, holding me when I sobbed and watching as I tried so desperately to find a place to belong in the religious community. I never found that place, because such a place does not exist.

Four years ago, out of the blue, my father called me and asked my partner and me to come over to visit—to have a BBQ. My partner and I agreed to go visit, armed with a code word to leave if we felt *the impending holy water shower coming on. The visit went great. My dad loved my partner, just as I knew he would. We now have a terrific relationship with my dad, but the encounter with my father's beliefs has shaped how I will raise my own daughter.*

I have decided to raise my daughter without religion. I decided not to allow the fear tactics of the church to dictate who and what my daughter will want to be when she grows up. I will not allow society's Christian views to smother her dreams and aspirations. I will not subject my daughter to the hurt, the tears, and the fears I experienced while being shunned by the church. In the end, as a mother, all I want for my child is for her to treat everyone she meets as she would want to be treated. I feel that if we all taught our children the Golden Rule without any sort of "God" attached, the world would be a much nicer place to live in.

Violence and Crime
and Emotional Health

No one is exempt from living in or around cruel behavior, so we teach our children how to cope. People who believe in God can pray that criminals receive the "ultimate justice," that there is some sort of fair deal worked out in the end: The criminal goes to hell; the victim goes to heaven. Believers can tell their kids that the Devil is the impetus behind evil acts and that God will take care of everything; he will right all wrongs. Of course, this takes the culpability of bad behavior away from the offender and pins it to an imaginary bad guy. If the offender desires to change, he must seek God to effect his transformation.

Some religions even believe that, no matter how often you sin, no matter what the crime, if you ask God for forgiveness, you will be saved. Exactly, how, I wonder, would you know if you're saved? How does God communicate this? And if you are getting the short end of the proverbial stick here on this planet—if you've been victimized, abused, or forsaken—these religions assure you not to worry, because God has a special plan for everyone. Everything will be fair after you die. If this doesn't make sense to you now, no worries—it does to God.

But that's not the way you and I think. We have to deal with the gritty reality here on earth. People can do mean things to each other. People can do horrible, awful things. How do we turn our gaze away from all that is bad in the world so that we can also appreciate what is good? It is important for us to teach our kids to find balance, so that they can enjoy what is good while being aware of what is bad, so that they don't become victims or victimizers.

Each day brings new crimes or tragedies, near and far. Late one afternoon, there were three helicopters circling a strip of woods behind my house. On the other side of the woods is a neighborhood not unlike mine, with families and people just like me going about their lives. When I saw the police chopper, I figured there had been another burglary.

But this time it was not. The helicopters circling behind our house were looking into the backyard of another house. A husband was suspected of murdering his wife, and he was burning something in his fire pit. I now know that two of the choppers were owned by news stations, hoping to get a glimpse of the husband burning his wife. But it turned out that it was not a body he was throwing into the fire. His wife was lying dead in the house. One of the couple's two kids found the mom. When the older child came home from school, she found the front door locked. Looking in the window, she saw her mom lying dead by the door. It makes you want to lay your head down on your arms: You've got to feel for that girl whose life was forever changed in those few moments. When there is a horrible crime, everyone suffers in a way, big or small. How does that happen?

What I dislike more than anything is telling my kids about the ugly underbelly of humankind. I don't know why this bothers me so much, because evil and violence have always been an inherent part of our existence. I think it's just because I want my kids to believe that people are innately good, especially the ones you choose to marry and have kids with. Yet I'd surely be setting them up to be taken advantage of—or worse—if they grew up believing that everyone has good intentions.

Evilness wears you down. Whether you believe in God or not, this sort of stuff is always hard to explain. People kill animals not just to eat, and sometimes they kill their own kind for reasons like revenge or for money or out of anger. The news brings us so many dirty details of so many crimes and so many criminals, yet with so little understanding of why they happen or how the seemingly friendly guy next door turns into a killing machine. At what point does affection turn to loathing?

So I told my sons what had happened when they asked. And my older son just shrugged his shoulders because he was already so used to hearing about horrific crimes that having one in our backyard was not shocking. My other son, a few years behind him, was still young enough to be shocked that a husband would kill his wife. What about the kids, he asked, were they okay? Why would someone do that? Before I could answer, my older son said, "Because people are selfish." His response reminded me of a George Carlin quote, "Inside every cynical person, there is a disappointed idealist." Perhaps he should have said: Inside every cynical person, there was once a trusting child.

Still, I tell my kids the truth—these acts of violence are neither normal nor typical, but the public's appetite for the sensational drives the media focus on these types of stories. They are not as widespread as they appear to be. Perhaps the reason we become fixated on bad news is simply because we do not understand the motives behind such crimes, and we are trying to figure out the missing link; perhaps it's because hearing about tragedies makes us appreciate that we are still breathing. I do not know. Yet even though we seem to constantly hear about these types of stories, our world is no more dangerous today than it was a hundred or a thousand years ago. We have more individual rights and more safety precautions in place now than in any other time in history. We just have to train our minds to look for and recognize what is good so that we don't focus on the sensational.

Young children need reassurance that Mom and Dad will keep them safe. They also need reassurance that the world is mostly a good place. A fellow blogger brought to my attention a story that Mr. Rogers used to tell about his mother. This is how she helped the young Fred deal with scary events: "My mother would say to me, 'Look for the helpers. You will always find people who are helping.' To this day, especially in times of 'disaster,' I remember my mother's words, and I am always comforted by realizing that there are still so many helpers—so many caring people in this world."[3]

There are a lot of people crawling over the face of this planet, yet only a small fraction of them do bad things, little and big. Sometimes it's an isolated incident like a murder or a drive-by shooting and sometimes it's a group of people victimizing another group, like the sex trade in Thailand. As nonbelievers, we can still hope that justice is served. Even though hoping is no more effective than praying, it still makes us feel as if we are part of a positive force.

It is also our responsibility to get involved if we can to avert a crime—or to come forward as a witness if we see one happening. There is no God watching and waiting to mete out justice. It's up to us to make sure justice is served so that our girls and boys can grow up to be women and men, mothers and fathers, and, eventually, grandparents.

We know, for example, that drunk drivers will be stopped by police, not God, so it's our duty to call 911 if we see that a driver is a threat. Caring that others are protected makes us human; it is the glue in our social contract that says, as part of society, we must strive to help our neighbors. That makes us feel empowered, that spreads good—and doing good makes us feel good, too.

We can help our children understand what a victim must feel: hurt, betrayed, forsaken, angry. None of us are exempt from pain and anguish, and, one day, inevitably, we will be the ones who need kindness from

---

[3] http://fci.org/new-site/par-tragic-events.html.

friends and family and even strangers. As nonbelievers, we're acutely aware that this is it; that we are it. We need each other, and the compassion that we can give to those who are suffering defines humanity. What can I do for my neighbors who have suffered a loss and need help? Pick up their children from school? Make a donation? Bring over a meal? Sometimes, just listening is the most important act of kindness.

While appreciating the positive and helping others are both important, our children also need to learn to create boundaries, to protect themselves from emotionally unhealthy people. They need to be emotionally healthy themselves, too. Our children should understand that within each of us lies the entire range of human emotions and possibilities. All of us have to ability to be good as well as evil. Children develop maturity by accepting emotions across the spectrum and learning how to process them. Teaching our children to talk about their fears and feelings, no matter how shocking to us, helps our kids label and get out into the open concerns that could otherwise become buried and toxic. We all have bad thoughts; for example, we all get angry. Expressing our anger—being heard and understood by the person whose actions prompted that anger—enables us to make the anger dissipate. Telling our children they shouldn't feel angry when they feel that emotion is not healthy—it doesn't make the feelings go away. It only makes children feel ashamed of their emotions, makes them hide how they're feeling, and fosters a great divide between how they feel and how they appear.

Emotional honesty is crucial for our children's mental health, for their self-esteem, and for their relationships. It is our job to help them attain this and to identify emotional honesty—or dishonesty—in others. I have seen adults who say they are not angry but who exhibit signs of anger, and I have taught my children to recognize this behavior as well. When someone says she is not mad, but slams a door, that passive-aggressive behavior is a symptom. And it means that, until she can communicate more openly, she will continue to cope with conflict in that unhealthy way. Most people who have unhealthy coping mechanisms do not become criminals, but happy, healthy relationships can only be forged by emotionally honest people.

We won't always be able to understand why some folks choose to do bad things. It's disappointing; it makes us sad, but we can recognize and avoid people who seem dangerous, who give us that feeling that something is not quite right. There are many people—so many people—who do good things every day. Little things that no one, no news station or newspaper, takes notice of. In a world in which we have no control, recognizing and participating in these small acts of kindness around us helps us have a more balanced perception of humanity. It's the best we can do. It is all we can do.

Sometimes Cheaters Win

It's hot as hell in Texas. This must be where the idea of Hades was conceived: one-hundred-plus degrees for days and days. Brown lawns. Dead flowers. Dried-up ponds. Scalding door handles.

My kid plays tennis in this heat every summer: academy, which means he's out there several hours a day. Then he goes on to high school tryouts for another three hours. At tryouts one day, I had to make a revision in my ideas of right and wrong.

It's wrong to cheat, right? For years I told my children, *Don't give people bad calls. When in doubt, do not call it out*. Give the other guy the benefit of the doubt. If your opponent gives you bad calls, sometimes that happens. Move on. It'll even out. But this time was different. My kid was a tenth-grader at the time, and he was playing a senior for the number-one spot. Being boys, it was a very competitive game. My kid was very small—a late bloomer. He was not even on the charts for weight. But he was the only freshman on the varsity team his first year. He worked hard.

So maybe the older and bigger kid should get the top spot because it's his last chance. But my son was determined. He and this boy were doubles partners last year, and I had watched the kid give a lot of bad calls. I told my son he should overrule the kid, but he wouldn't do it. Partners don't do that. Coaches don't like that.

Now he was the boy's opponent. The kid was no different playing my son. Several of the balls were so obviously in bounds, and I felt just really disheartened watching. Finally, my son went up to the net and questioned the call. The kid said, "I saw it out. It's my call. Too bad." I could tell my kid was getting stressed. He was up 4–1. The set continued and, just as I suspected, he lost his composure—and the set—at 5–7. After the match, I heard the boys on the bleachers. My son told the other kid he didn't play fair. I heard the kid laugh and say, "You have two more years. I'm a senior. This is my last chance."

This is a difficult life lesson—for me and for my kid. What do I tell him? Sorry, but you know he is your friend and he's a senior. This is sort of fair, too, in a democratic way. Do I tell him to forgive his friend for cheating? Should I tell him, just forget about it—move on? I think we all have it in us to cheat; some of us just have an easier time of it than others.

What I told my son—and some may not agree—was to give the kid a bad call back after three clearly bad calls. I thought about how many times I told him to ignore bad behavior. Now I was making him vindictive and vengeful. I just thought that I had to teach him to stand up for himself, even if it meant compromising his values. There were no line judges and no other solutions. Sometimes cheaters do win.

Do we take it or fight back? I think that's a tough call for the religious and the nonreligious alike. When is being wrong, right?

New Drivers: Creating a Healthy Conscience

The first time your kid has a fender bender, it's pretty unnerving. My son's first time was in the parking lot at the tennis courts (his first time for a fender bender, I mean). His friends were throwing tennis balls at his truck, and he wasn't paying attention. He was looking at them while backing up and, luckily, he didn't run over anyone; he only backed into a car.

So, of course, he called me, afraid that I would be angry. *What should I do?* He was clearly upset. I said, *Go into the office and ask the front desk if they know whose car it is. You have to tell the owner.*

He told me that the only people who saw him hit the car were his two friends. They agreed it was a very small dent, about the size of a fist, and it was on the bumper. The impact was so small, he said, that there was no damage to his truck.

I knew that he was trying to jockey me into exonerating him, into telling him, *It's probably no big deal. You can leave.* And, trust me, I was rolling my eyes and wondering how much this was going to raise his insurance.

He was afraid of that, too. He is very money-conscious. He also knew that, if he ever got a ticket, he'd pay for his insurance, and he was struggling just to fill the old clunker with gas.

He reminded me that some guy had backed into the side of my car, leaving a $1,200 dent—and he didn't leave any note.

I told him, *Go inside and ask whose car it is*. After a few minutes, I got another call saying that the guy at the desk didn't know. I could hear it in my son's voice—here was yet another reason for him to leave, as fast as he could, before anyone else saw him.

Leave a note, I said, w*ith your insurance information and our phone number. Put it under the other car's windshield wiper.*

So that's what he did. I stayed on the phone while he wrote everything down.

A couple of days, then a week went by, and no one called. He was relieved. Perhaps the owner thought it was no big deal. Perhaps it was a rental car he hit, and it didn't matter.

But then he got a call from the insurance company. And, yes, the kid had been honest. The dent was so small that it would come out of the deductible and his premium would not be raised. He was relieved.

I told him, had he left, he would forever have in his memory that he didn't do the right thing. He would have committed a crime not only against another person, but also against his own conscience. There are a lot people who would have left and never looked back. But he didn't want to be one of them.

The most important thing, I told him, is who you are when no one is looking.

Letting Go:
When Children Leave

My older son is now a senior and will leave for college in the fall. I've already told him that if he sees me crying he should just ignore me. I am sad that he's taking flight, but I'm also happy that he will have the chance to go off on his own and experience college. I'll get over it.

If you have kids, I'm sure you remember the day when your son or daughter was born, that day you held your baby and saw the perfect little fingers with perfect little nails. My son looked like ET when he arrived on the scene. And he didn't cry, not a peep. I thought he was dead. The nurses and doctor worked on him, and then rushed him away. I was so relieved when they brought him in and placed him in my arms. He craned his long neck and looked around. I couldn't believe that, in nine months, I had made him with the food I'd eaten.

That was my kid's first big exit . . . or should I say it was his first big entrance into this world? Now, he's ready to make his next big exit—or entrance. I hope when he walks out our door to college, he will be safe and self-assured. I know he will work hard, and I hope he will find the right kids to hang with. But I think I will worry just the same—that's where belief in God would probably be a comfort. If I could just ask someone with more power than me to watch over him, to make sure he's safe when he walks the campus at night or goes to parties with his buddies. When you believe in God, there's always someone who can look out for your kids—dead relatives, guardian angels, Jesus. When you don't believe, you rely on your kid's abilities and the kindness of strangers.

When your kid goes off to college, it's like losing someone you love. And, in a sense, you do. A child leaves and an adult comes back. For now, I just try to spend every minute I can with him. I don't complain about socks left on the floor or an unmade bed. All those things are minor. He works hard in school and in his sport. He is respectful. I want him to have good recollections of his childhood. I don't want to leave him with final memories of me pestering him to make his bed as he rushes out at 7 a.m. to get to school for an early meeting.

As parents we become acutely aware that life is just one long series of letting-go moments. We start missing our kids right away, almost as soon as they are born: We miss their baby smell and their soft, fleshy legs; we miss their wobbly heads and startle reflex; we miss their helplessness; we miss seeing them crawl; we miss seeing their six-month-old clothes with farm animal decorations; we miss their toothless smiles and their giggles; we miss that they used to talk to us about every new friend or say silly things. We miss their training wheels, the picture books we read to them at night, the children's museums, the hiking trails where they picked flowers for us, the Disney movies with adult innuendos. We miss them looking to us for the answers and getting excited about things like fish in a tank and shooting stars and hugs from Mom and Dad. But with every sweet moment we add to our mind's memory chest, the time we have with our children drains away. Our kids become increasingly mobile and independent, both in body and mind, and if we're lucky, if we're doing our job right, we will miss our kids and they will miss us, but we will all be able to let go.

Letting go, though, doesn't mean that the worry leaves when our kids do. Julie, who is atheist, has a daughter who moved far away from home to attend college. Not only does she feel concern for her daughter's safety when she is away, but she also feels isolated being a nonbeliever in a very religious community in Montana. She says, "When you don't have the belief that there is a higher power looking over and protecting your child through prayer as she ventures out into the big world, it does make a parent feel helpless. I've taught my kids to always be aware of their surroundings and to try to make wise decisions, but kids with or without the belief in God have the mentality of being superhuman and that nothing bad will happen to *them*. What scares me is the concept of my child being with people of religious faith who truly think God is watching over them—that their judgment may be impaired because they honestly imagine a higher power protecting them and thus end up putting themselves, along with my child, at risk or in danger. The mentality that praying to the invisible guy in the sky automatically gives that person protection makes me believe that they would tend to be more careless individuals and not as cautious as those of us without that belief."

When Julie expressed her concerns about her daughter's safety to her brother-in-law, he replied, "Well, all you can do is pray that nothing happens to her." As nonbelievers, there is the added frustration of not being able to connect with other parents. You and I can't wave off our concerns and give God our proxy. We know that the only people who will watch out for our kids are other people. Sometimes, we can't even rely on them.

TEACHERS

· AND ·

PEERS

Let's Teach Religion
in the Classroom

C omparative religion classes do help foster religious tolerance. Konsta, who is raising his two children without religion in Finland, shared this with me: "Our kids have never been church members but both have attended religious classes at school. The classes are not about the dogma but more what you'd call comparative religion. Being tolerant is the reason we decided that it would be good for them to attend the classes. Our son switched to philosophy at seventh grade and our daughter can choose for herself as well in a few years. I would say that one of the biggest reasons for general tolerance has been our educational system. One can get a postgrad degree without having to pay basically a dime. Universal health care is also a point worth mentioning. Schooling and taking care of illnesses will not bankrupt anyone."

This is not the case in the land of the free. A college education may be prohibitively expensive. And comparative religion courses are not taught in elementary or middle schools. However, there are a lot of references to God and Christianity in our schools, from both teachers and peers.

You might think that I don't want religion taught in our public schools, that I would not want it taught to my children. Yet I do. I think that religion, being such an important part of our culture, should be an important part of our education, too. Teachings of all major religions, along with explanations of nonreligious worldviews, both ancient and modern, would enrich and open our children's minds. Required religion courses—integrated with history and presented in an objective and factual way—might be just the thing we need to raise tolerant, critical thinking citizens.

One lesson I learned when my kids went off to elementary school was that talk of God could not be kept off the playground or out of the classroom. Students in my younger son's class, mere first-graders, often spoke to him about Jesus, angels, and the Devil. I also found that my older son's teacher and peers sometimes talked about God and religion during class. And, on a regular basis, I watched as my son's coach gathered the team in a circle to pray before the game.

Clearly, our psyche is not compartmentalized; we cannot strain our religious beliefs out of our thoughts, ideas, and perceptions. Our faith as individuals and as a nation shapes our laws and is the seed of many controversial issues: abortion, gay marriages, embryonic stem-cell research. Since religion is so ubiquitous, we might as well acknowledge it and give it a place to hang its hat in the classroom.

There is much we can learn. History is spattered far and wide with the wrongs committed in the name of God or by mortals who have usurped the powers supposedly reserved for deities. On the other hand, although religion is not a science, it is not quantifiable, and it is not based on logic, it is a creative construct that has served our nation well at times. It has provided hope and solace as well as a moral framework for many of our citizens. Religion's history, ideas, and prominent leaders have a great deal to offer, so it behooves us to study and to understand.

In learning about other worldviews, we promote tolerance, encourage harmony, and come to a greater understanding of all people, past and present.

Perhaps some will oppose this idea because they want religion in schools only on their own terms, in line with their own faiths. Yet we are not the same country we once were—we're no longer a small sect of Christians escaping religious persecution. The melting pot is bigger, the soup more diverse.

It starts with our children, in the classroom. In order to fairly represent and understand all the individuals in our communities, there should be a place in our schools for teaching all religious and nonreligious worldviews. This way we can grow tolerant, open-minded, critical thinkers. I want my children to understand other religious views on their way to finding their own.

God in School:
Teachers Who Recruit

You just never know if your child's teacher will be a classroom preacher. A few years ago, my older son had a really good fifth-grade math teacher, Mrs. P. Unfortunately, Mrs. P also talked about religion in class. A lot. Had she talked about magical spells or Devil-worshipping or atheism, I'm sure she would have been fired. Let's be honest: Christian parents would have knocked down the school doors and dragged the teacher out by her hair the first few days of school.

My son and I had many discussions about religious talk in class. When your kid is able to detect inappropriate God-speak, you know you're winning the cultural battle. But one Friday, Mrs. P took things too far. She went around the room and asked the students to tell the class where they went to church on Sundays. When she got to my kid, not yet realizing the magnitude of his words or that we were outliers, he simply told her that our family doesn't go to church. We're agnostics. I wish I could have been there to see her face: She had found a soul to save in the land of Stepford Baptists.

So she asked the class to talk to their parents and see if any of them could go to our house on Sunday, pick up my son, and take him to church with their family. I don't know why I didn't go in and immediately speak with her. I was mistaken—I believed I was being tolerant. My son had simply told her, "No, thanks." There didn't seem to be a need to confront her. She was a competent teacher, and I didn't want to rock the proverbial boat. Yet Mrs. P was really undermining me as a parent: She was teaching my son that I wasn't doing a good job responding to his "spiritual" needs. The more I thought about it, the more I realized the message she was sending to my kid was not a good one. So a few days later, I went in and talked with the principal, who also happened to be a member of the largest Baptist church in town.

If you're like me, you're probably thinking of all the potential repercussions of talking with a teacher's boss. Will it hurt your kid in the classroom? Will he get lower grades? Will the teacher continue to proselytize, but on a more subtle level? But I had to stop the religious recruitment or my son would be subject to it all year. So I talked with the principal and told her my concerns about Mrs. P. I said that I did not have a problem with teaching religion in the classroom—as long as *all* the world's major religions were presented and taught in an objective way, during a specific time set aside for that topic. I even offered to talk with the school district about adding a comparative religion component to the curriculum.

The principal nodded her head and said okay, she would talk with Mrs. P. I had the feeling she thought I was a nutcase. (Though at least I didn't levitate and spew green vomit.) And, realistically, many of the people we encounter—at least in my town—not only feel that it's acceptable to talk about their religion but that it's their duty to evangelize and to bring the unchurched "home." That's when it becomes *our* duty to advocate for our kids from a rational perspective. We're not looking to keep God and religion out altogether—let's be real. The Bible has many stories that make for interesting study. Religion is inextricably braided into the fabric of our history, art, and literature. We just don't want religious recruitment or favoritism—and it's never acceptable to preach in class.

As nonbelievers, we want what is fair for all of us. If we want tolerance, we have to give that, too. The goal is to make our children aware of teachers who try to sell their faith so that our sons and daughters can communicate this to us. If the teacher talks about her church in class: not OK. If the teacher asks your children what church they attend: not OK. If the teacher tells the class that Christianity has had a major influence in the shaping of our nation: OK.

It's not just the South or the Midwest that has these issues. Parents have written to me from all over the country with concerns that teachers are using their authority to try to influence students into believing that it is wrong not to go to church or believe in a supreme being. While our kids are young, it is our responsibility to recognize and deal with it. If your child's teacher crosses the line, go early and often to clear the air. After my talk with the principal, my son's teacher did stop the overt recruiting. She knew she had a pair of ears in class that would hold her accountable.

On the Playground

If your children are preschool-aged, they will most likely never have to worry about losing a friend over views about God or religion or politics. It's not the kids we have to worry about, but the parents who talk as the kids are playing in the sandbox. Mothers and fathers are very protective of their young, and especially when they are young, parents tend to be militant about monitoring what children are fed, both through their mouths and ears. Naturally, a father who is raising his daughter to be Methodist would not want his youngster hearing words that contradict his belief system. It's sort of like telling a young child there is no Santa Claus. I know about this one myself—because I believed. I really did. I was just five when my Jewish friend broke the news to me. I was stunned—I did not try to argue with her. What she said made sense. "Do you really think there's a man who goes to all of our houses in one night and climbs in through the chimney?" My mother, however, was ticked. My little friend had ruined it for all of us. My mother believed it was her place to pull back the curtain on Santa. Yet I think if kids knew the truth—that Santa is Mom and Dad—they'd still be just as excited to wake up at 4:30 in the morning on Christmas day and open gifts. What kid wouldn't be? Kids don't care where the presents come from, just as long as there are toys under the tree.

But I digress. There exists a problem for nonbelievers on the playground, as evidenced by one of the many comments I've received. One mom from Oregon wrote:

> *Once, while at a park with my children, I encountered another mother. Our children were playing well together, and we began a friendly chat. We were in agreement on most things and seemed to really hit it off until we came to the topic of religion. She revealed that she was Christian, and she obviously wanted to know my beliefs. I told her I was agnostic. Immediately she looked at me as though I had sprouted horns, called her children away from mine, and went to the other side of the park without offering so much as a good-bye.*

> *I try to live a moral and kind life. It is my hope that people are surprised out of their stereotypical ways of thinking when they learn of my agnosticism. Unfortunately, though, more often than not, they are unable to see past their ingrained beliefs.*

I feel for this mom, trying to reach out and connect with another parent—only to be treated as if she had a communicable disease. The problem is, we're not the ones who are affected as much as our kids are. We're adults, and we understand that we can be a threat to some people. Those parents who are raising kids with religion *can't* allow doubt in their lives. One elementary school teacher shared with me that revealing she was an atheist would definitely get her fired. No parent would want her to teach young children out of the fear that her views would slip out in class because children believe whatever you tell them.

One dad said this:

I don't usually feel the need to justify my secular life. If eternal damnation is my destination after I die, that affects me and me only. There's really no point in debating it, and I don't even feel the need to defend my beliefs on that account. But it does strike a chord with me when someone suggests that we can have no morality without God. My brother and I were both raised in a secular household, and while neither of us is perfect, we both grew up to be ethical human beings and achieve success on our own terms. We, coincidentally, both went into fields of service to others. I am a police officer. On a daily basis, I go into homes decorated with crucifixes, rosaries, and Virgin Mary statuettes, and I arrest husbands and wives who beat each other while their children play amid a mess of empty liquor bottles and trays of drugs and drug paraphernalia. At the end of the shift, I come home to my house with no crucifixes or mezuzot, but also no domestic violence or drug abuse.

As nonbelievers, you and I know that religious belief reveals nothing about our morality. So what do we have to do until the rest of the nation understands this, too? If your kid is having fun and getting along well in the sandbox, you could try one of the following:

- Decline to reveal your thoughts on religion. Offer instead, "Oh, I don't talk about religion or politics or childbirth horror stories." Parents might be a little taken aback, but they probably won't pick up their progeny and run off.

- Pretend you didn't hear the question and divert the other parent's attention to another topic. "What do you think about that new charter school that just opened up?"

On the other hand, if your child's playmate has just pushed your daughter to the ground for the third time, and you think, "I will not let my child be used as a Bobo doll again," then you should feel free to tell the other parent how you really feel (about religion, that is).

What to Tell Classmates

Growing up outside mainstream religion is tough. Nastia L., who is now an atheist, wrote:

I grew up in a Jewish family in the South, and it was almost as bad as being an atheist. I got no end of people pushing their brand of Christianity on me, or people hating me for not being Christian—neighborhood parents telling their kids not to play with me because "all Jews go to hell" and the kids crying to me, begging me to be "saved" so we can all just play again. Oh, and not being allowed to be friends with Muslims was even better (sarcasm). In my life, religion poisoned everything. I escaped the South in the nineties and I've been an atheist for many years now, and it's wonderful. Having lived in Europe and in other parts of the United States was eye-opening. We're not the freaks they make us out to be in the South; we're just fine.

If you live in an area of the country where Christianity reigns supreme, growing up may be difficult. I've taught my kids (as many nonbelievers have) to be tolerant and respectful of others' religions, but this courtesy is not always extended to us, at least, not at this point in our nation's movement toward tolerance of all worldviews. Our children are already aware of this, as one mom pointed out: "I was talking to my eleven-year-old daughter the other night and told her that I suspect many people who claim to be religious do it to fit in rather than go against the grain. She very honestly stated that she would probably pretend just to avoid all the hate. I can't say I blame her."

It wasn't until middle school that religion became a hot topic for my older child with his friends. Kids would ask him what church he belonged to, and when my son explained that we're agnostics, they called him a Devil-worshipper or tried to argue him back into belief. He lost friends; he was an outsider. Christians, for all their talk about goodness and kindness and not judging, are some of the most judgmental people I know.

I've found that raising kids without religion becomes easier the older they get. My older son is now in twelfth grade, and he's learned not to participate in religious conversation or to just say, "I don't like to talk about it." That works for him because he's pretty soft-spoken anyway.

I learned from kid #1. When kid #2 came along, I told him he could handle God questions several ways. He's the kind of child who needs to fit in, and it's a common desire for preteens and teenagers to be similar, not different, from their peers. Other parents have written me to say that their kids are wary of letting friends know that they are not believers. Fitting in at school is important, and they don't want to stand out.

One mom, who identified herself as a humanist, said that she's trying to teach her kids to be assertive in their humanism. But when her son, age ten, is asked about his religious preference, he tells people that he's half Jewish and half Christian but doesn't go to temple or church. Her middle school–aged child considers it "social suicide" to tell people she doesn't believe in God, so she keeps very quiet about it.

Honesty is very important because we are our words, and we want to teach our children to uphold the value of our language. We want our kids to be honest and real. On the other hand, I also believe that we don't always have to make full disclosure if the question is (1) nobody's business or (2) going to harm them or someone else. Our country is still very polarized, and I don't want our kids (yours and mine) to have the nation's religious fight on their shoulders. For younger kids (like my son), finessing the question seems to work. We've told him that he can say, "My grandmother is Catholic." That stops people from evangelizing, it's the truth, and it helps him fit in. They just assume that the rest of the family is, too. I also told him he could always blame me: "My mom told me not to talk about religion." Then change the subject. Parents always make good scapegoats. (From Leviticus 16 [as noted in *Merriam-Webster*]: *Scapegoat. A goat sent into the wilderness after the Jewish chief priest had symbolically laid the sins of the people upon it.*) My kid prefers the former option, but your children may like placing the blame on you.

This stance might seem like a cop-out, but if you have kids in middle and/or high school, you know there's a lot of pressure to fit in. There will come a time when they will be ready to speak up and say, "I'm a nonbeliever" or "I prefer not to talk about it." There may also come a time when nonbelievers receive the respect and tolerance that the religious receive. But don't worry. Until then, you're kids will still know what they're doing and who they are. My sons often come home from school with stories to tell and hypocrisies noted. Kids learn fast that actions don't always match the dogma taught in church. My younger son will often say, "And so-and-so says he's a Christian. That's not how Christians are supposed to act."

■

CRYSTAL'S STORY: WHAT SHE TELLS HER CHILDREN ABOUT CHURCH

Crystal lives in Texas and is raising her son without religion:

My son came home from school one day after a fellow student had convinced him that he needed to go to church. She was following in her parents' footsteps, believing it was her duty to spread the word, and I'm sure she has a lot of fun there. Since my son was only eight, I hadn't felt compelled to lay it all out for him yet about why we don't go to church because it had never been pitched to him in such an exciting way before. When religious discussions are brought home from either friends or Scouts, I make it a point to compare it to and relate it with all the world's other religions. I told him that we can visit churches and hear their messages, but with hundreds of religions out there it would take us years. How would we ever decide on one? My hope is that he makes the same connection that I did as a child. My belief in the fairy tales started to unravel when I asked the right questions and discovered there were many versions of God, and believing in just this one God determined your eternal fate. My BS detector went crazy, but it still took me years to come to terms with the idea that you don't HAVE to believe and that it was OK. I'm hoping that since my son has a mother who will accept whatever his heart believes, he will not have the same hurdles against whatever feels right.

Bad Babies

Maybe optimism isn't always a good thing.

My kid read *Lord of the Flies* in his middle school class. After the class was finished reading the book, the teacher took a survey. She asked the students if they thought children were born good or bad. In a class of twenty-two, only two said that babies were born neither good nor bad. The rest said that, yes, children are born "bad." They are born sinful or with "original sin." None said babies were born good. One student said that if a child was given the choice between a good action and a bad action, he will choose the bad one every time.

Wow. It's scary that almost every student had been led to believe that babies—not knowing language or morality—are born "bad." Middle school students are old enough to think for themselves, but their brains are frozen into certain patterns of thought already. They don't understand that the universe is not moral or immoral, that definitions of *sinful, good,* and *bad* are human-made. The universe doesn't discriminate, doesn't judge. Neither do babies.

I tried to imagine what the world must be like for the students who believe that we are innately bad. Are they suspicious of everyone's motives? Are they fearful of strangers? Then I realized that is what politicians prey on: America's innate fear of the "other" and of the unknown. And I wondered, if I surveyed the more rational folks who read this, how many were "scared into" supporting the Iraq war in 2003? How many were waiting for some substantive justification for going to war?

Perhaps I put my kid at a disadvantage by not making him more fearful or suspicious. He is not "on guard" for the bad that could happen. Yes, he might be more optimistic about human nature and the world around him, but he might be easier prey with his willingness to trust. He could end up being a sucker or a victim.

Taking God's Thunder
versus Taking Life

I n my son's ninth-grade English class, the students had an interesting discussion. They were talking about morality. These ninth-graders were pretty sophisticated thinkers, at least I thought they were. But I was floored by what my kid told me. In rating different crimes or actions, most of the class ranked "taking God's name in vain" above "killing another human being." He talked with a classmate about why the boy ranked his choices like this. The boy said, "God created everything. He gave us life. Killing is just harming one person."

How have we raised our children to believe that it is more harmful to take God's name in vain than to take the life of another human being? You have to wonder if these kids have given any thought to what it means to take the Lord's name in vain. Did the phrase *goddamnit* exist when the Ten Commandments were written? I don't think so. More likely it meant that you shouldn't use God's name to manipulate people. Don't try to steal his thunder and make yourself into the Lord's mini-me. Don't speak on his behalf—just like the thousands of people you hear every day saying, "God wants this" or "God would be disappointed about that," especially preachers who seem to know the intimate details of God's ethereal mind. Hell, I can barely understand my own mind or my kids', so the concept of another human being able to tap into God's innermost thoughts seems doubtful to me at best.

If these students believe now, on their way to adulthood, that appropriating God's name is worse than killing another person, will these kids ever be able to ascend Lawrence Kohlberg's stages of moral development? Or will they forever be stuck in stage 2, bending to the nonexistent will of an imaginary being, conforming to a Bible that they think should be law for everyone?

Are We Smarter than
a Sixth-Grader?:
Fear of the Unknown

Fear is a big motivator. Several years ago, my son came home with this question: Will the world end in 2012? Seems this was the topic du jour in his sixth-grade biology class. We do live in Texas, so naturally these sorts of questions merit serious consideration.

The teacher told the students not to listen to "that mumbo jumbo about the world ending." And I was glad to hear about her enlightened response. You just never know what sort of character will roll into your kids' classrooms every year. But the problem wasn't the teacher. My son said several kids insisted it was true. Swore to it. The world would definitely and without any doubt end in 2012. All believers would immediately be taken to heaven, abandoning their moving cars and their helpless, unsaved pets. The nonbelievers (heathens, Devil-worshippers) would be left behind to loot and live lasciviously. Naturally, to a sixth-grader, this was a little confusing.

My son had a problem on his hands. Should he believe his friends or his teacher? Fortunately, I was the tiebreaker. I told him there have been a lot of times throughout history when civilizations predicted that the world would end. People were afraid of a catastrophic occurrence at the turn of the twenty-first century. Did he remember anything about that year, when he had been the ripe old age of three? He thought for a minute. I said, *We're still here, right?*

"But how do you know for sure something won't happen?" he asked.

I don't, I told him. *No one does.* We don't know what will happen next year or even tomorrow, though we can make a good guess based on what happened yesterday and in the last year and in the year before that. That unpredictability, however, makes life exciting, but it also leaves the door open for misinterpretation, gambling, and fear mongering. The ancient Mayans certainly could not predict what would happen thousands of years in the future—and they weren't even trying to predict the end of the world. Heck, they didn't even have computers, televisions, or calculators.

The irony is this: So many folks hyperventilated over the possibility that the world would suddenly end, yet they felt no fear over the true dangers we face: gun violence, climate change, low-level ozone, water-quality issues, energy shortages, nuclear weapons.

It seems that we struggle to understand and react to the real dangers around us, but it's very easy for us to react to fear of the unknown.

Are we smarter than sixth-graders?

Intelligent Design:
A Misnomer?

I t's odd that some folks in the state where I live think "Intelligent Design" is an intelligent counter to evolution. Or that it is even intelligent. The universe is, if I may borrow a term from my Christian friends, a miracle (meaning a highly improbable or extraordinary event). It's mysterious, amazing, awe-inspiring, but "intelligent" or "designed"—perhaps not. There is no evidence of a plan or forethought. We wouldn't have species evolving if the "design" had been well thought-out, if it had been right the first time. For that matter we would not have flux, or even time, since time is simply the expansion of the universe into space. No, we are still moving and changing, and there are no speed limits, stop signs, or indications of a destination. I see no evidence of a blueprint or an intelligent designer. And as creatures that came along billons of years after the universe was created, how would we even know what the original design was? Perhaps the planets were supposed be connected in a ring around the sun, with life on every planet, and you and I were meant to have wings.

Only from our human-centric point of view could we believe that one man ("Adam") was perfectly created. We are imperfect machines, susceptible to mental and physical illnesses, fatigue, age, bacteria, viruses, fungi, heat, cold, gravity, and the jaws of bigger and stronger predators. Our bodies have design flaws, imperfections, redundancies, and inefficiencies. We carry within our cells loads of genetic baggage, genes that are vulnerable to small changes in our environment, which can be switched on to create a myriad of cancers and diseases and birth defects. We share 60 percent of the same genes with the lowly fruit fly and 96 percent of the same genes as apes, reducing our "uniqueness" to a mere 4 percent of special programming.

We are miraculous only because we are so adaptive, and if being adaptive is suggestive of anything, it suggests that we do not have an original, intelligent designer. Rather, what we truly are is lucky. You and I and our kids are the "chosen ones" because, of all possible egg and sperm combinations, we got the chance to make an entrance on life's stage at a time in history when we have consciousness, when we can use language to label our feelings, travel to places that early humans could not, and sleep in a clean, warm bed, safe from hungry animals.

Intelligent Design calls itself a scientific theory, yet it is just another way of saying, "I don't understand, but I know God had something to do with it." This is not a new battle: Many men (and women, to a much lesser extent) have spent over two hundred years trying to fit science and religion together like pieces of a puzzle. So it's no surprise that Intelligent Design is used as a subterfuge to bring religion, particularly Christianity, into the classroom. Our need to have answers to questions we don't yet understand, that are beyond our abilities to figure out, makes us willing to settle for explanations that are unsupported. That is the easy way.

It's okay to teach kids that we don't have to have all the answers. We don't have to create—or adopt—a creation narrative to fill in the blanks or explain how we got here. Our understanding of the universe is still in its infancy, and as we age as a species, if we continue as a species, we will change and adjust our sense of what we previously thought was true or correct. We don't need to prostitute knowledge or bend it to our will just so that we can arrive at conclusions that will comfort us. Our greatest challenge comes in being comfortable with the unknown, in reflecting on the information we have, and in keeping our minds open to our continuously shifting understanding of ourselves and the universe.

At this point in time, God is a wish. God is a guess. God is only a hypothesis.

Sleepover

I should've known it would be a long night. My kid, who was celebrating his eleventh birthday, warned me that one of his friends has ADHD. "But he takes his medication—most of the time," my son said, "even though he doesn't like to."

It's OK, I told him. *Everything will be fine.* I'm not a strong believer in medicating kids—I always wonder about the ADD/ADHD thing. After all, when most of us were in school, no students took medication to make them concentrate or to calm them down. If you were rowdy, you went to the principal's office. Your mom came in and/or you were paddled. That had a way of fixing your behavior, albeit not in a way that we would now consider humane.

But I digress. This boy, whom I'll call "Timmy," was the first to arrive. He spent the first hour at my house screaming at the top of his lungs and running around as if his pants were on fire. He was wired. I had an image of his mother, smiling as she drove away as fast as she could. It was Saturday night. I looked longingly at the wine bottle in my refrigerator and wished I could pop open the cork and have a few swigs.

This was going be a long night, I knew. I'm not very good when it comes to sleepover parties. Boys are loud, and I'm quiet. A lot of wild activity, and I start feeling frazzled. My mind tries to concentrate on all the different noises at once. I become dazed and confused.

My plan was to take the boys for pizza and then for a couple of hours of laser tag at Main Event, one of those family entertainment centers. Timmy loaded up on the soda, but ate very little. (I cursed those all-you-can-drink soda fountains.) When it came time to play laser tag, he didn't want to play. He came over and asked me for money for tokens. *OK*, I said, *I'll buy everyone some tokens for the night, but when they're gone, that's it.* Timmy used his immediately. He took the tickets he'd won on the games and went to the prize counter. Next thing I knew, he was banging his fists on the glass display cases, shouting, "Get over here and help me!!!" My son thought it was funny. I gave him the look. I told the kid he'd sit out if he did that again. He smirked and said, "OK."

Timmy went to join the other boys for laser tag. About fifteen minutes later, I found that he had sneaked out of the arena and was stealing tickets out of one of the games. By the time I found him, he had taken over four hundred tickets. I returned the tickets to the employee at the counter and just offered a meek "sorry." I took Timmy back into the laser tag arena and stood guard by the door. Later I found he wasn't really in there playing laser tag but running full steam into other kids, trying to plow them over. I would have laughed if I weren't the parent responsible for the urchin.

Before we left for the night, Timmy wanted something to drink. *Sure*, I said, *but only water. It's too late for soda.*

"Then I don't want anything," he said. So we left.

Timmy was loud the whole night, in spite of my requests for the kids to quiet down. *The other kids*, I told him at midnight, *want to sleep.* He stayed awake until after 3 a.m., playing with the handheld electronics he had brought from home. I drifted in and out of sleep, awakened by his periodic outbursts of laughter or grunts. I dreamed of Jane Eyre and wild animals and caves. Or, at least, I thought I did.

The boys were up and going strong by 8:00 a.m. I made them breakfast. Timmy got OJ to drink but wanted Dr Pepper, which, he told us, he always drinks for breakfast (and lunch). *We don't buy soda*, I said, *Sorry.* Timmy was disappointed. He continued to eat his food using—no exaggeration—his fingers to cut and eat his waffles.

Fruit? I asked him. "I'm not really a fruit guy," he said. I smiled and nodded; okay. He played with his bacon and made one long smear of pig grease for a landing atop the table—eleven and still making airplanes out of bacon. The kid had no manners. He never once said *thank you.*

Why did I tell you about my night? To show you that I have a lot to work on when it comes to being a fun mom? (True.) To show you how selfish I was for wanting my kids' birthday celebration to be over? (True.) No, I have another reason.

This kid—Timmy—was a fifth-grader and the son of a teacher at my kid's school. As moms and dads, we hear criticisms from society about what we feed our kids and how we neglect to teach our children manners, how discipline in the classroom is such a huge problem because of the way we parent—or don't parent. Yet raising kids is not such an easy thing, even for a teacher.

Timmy was picked up promptly at 10:00 a.m. so he could go to church with his mom. She called me on my cell phone to say that she was waiting outside in the car. All I could think as I watched the kid walk to the minivan was this: thank GOD. I would have smiled as they drove off had I not been so damn tired.

Please Don't Ask
God for a Win

I t was cold, near freezing. I stood with my hands deep in my pockets
for warmth, watching my kid run onto the soccer field. He was ten.
His arms and legs were like noodles, and he was by far the smallest
and skinniest boy on the team. I worried that he'd be picked on or
pushed around. But when I talked to him, I knew that he had incredible
inner strength. He would fight if pushed. He would not be bullied. I
don't know where he got that strength, but I'm pretty sure it wasn't
from an almighty power.

I watched the boys taking turns kicking balls at the goalie. They
were little mini-men, all dressed in royal blue shorts, shirts, and socks.
Coach came on the field. Coach was the kind of guy who, when he looked
at you, didn't look you directly in the eye. He looked at the ground or
askance. He turned his head and cocked it slightly, as if he were listening
to someone else at the same time he was having a conversation with you.
He had no children on this team. He had no boys of his own. He coached
on behalf of his church. Many of the boys here were at-risk youth, he told
me. This team needed to be saved.

Coach waved the boys over, and they huddled together on the side of the field. I know what they are doing. Before every game, they bow their heads and pray. Here is what Coach asks for: good weather, the ability to play their best, and, of course, a win. Lord Jesus is invoked at every soccer game. On this day, I wonder, will Jesus bring us a win or will he help my neighbor who is recovering from a stroke? I think about approaching Coach after the game and asking him this: "If your God is so powerful, why are you praying for something as pointless as a soccer game?" I think about telling Coach that I don't want my son to be part of his silly little prayer group. I think about telling him that religion is mostly a collection of self-serving belief systems that do more harm than good.

But I don't. I accept this quietly because religion is one of the big topics that even children get worked up over. I don't want people to think I don't respect their belief system, nor do I not want Coach to set his sights on converting my son and me. Sometimes it's better to be silent if you won't be understood.

How to Handle
Prayer Groups

Tolerance means a willingness to allow for the existence of behavior or opinions that one does not necessarily agree with. You and I know that, as nonbelievers, we aren't always granted the tolerance we accord others. Yet we must still teach our children tolerance. Why? you might ask. Because tolerance means you are being fair, that you are being as objective as possible, and these are traits that we want our children to have, even if others are not quite there yet.

Last spring, I was sitting in the bleachers, waiting for my kid's tennis team to start playing. I was snack mom: I brought the players chips and beer. No, just kidding. I brought age-appropriate snacks. Before the matches began, one of the kids, "Joshua," called the team together, joined hands and began to pray. This kid knew his Bible verses better than any preacher I've heard, citing Corinthians, and praying like a professional.

He asked God to be present at their match, to help the team get the win they deserve and have worked hard for. I bit my lip and, of course, wanted to say, "Shouldn't we be asking for world peace or more jobs so our citizens don't have to live on the streets?" But I didn't. Because that kid was only doing what he'd been taught, and that is to ask God for stuff. Speaking up and shaming him would only embarrass and humiliate all the kids who believed as he did.

I could have approached the coach and made an issue. Was it worth it? Probably not. It turns out, as I discovered recently, the coach came to understand that she had a religiously diverse team and wanted to be more sensitive to others anyway. Sometimes, forcing one's hand just makes things worse.

But it was a good lesson for my kid and me. My son looked over and raised his eyebrows. I knew what he was thinking, and he knew what I was thinking. Yeah, it's crazy and we think that prayer is silly, but you've got to show respect for others' belief systems. I gave him a straight face. He knew better than to laugh or smirk. My son could have chosen not to join the team prayer, but it's awkward to be the only member of the team who declines to participate.

After the match, I made sure to draw a parallel between the tennis prayer circle and the crazy preacher in Florida who wanted to burn the Quran. The preacher showed extreme disrespect and intolerance for Islam, and we have to be careful, as nonbelievers, not to show disrespect or intolerance for others' beliefs. Yes, "Joshua" was sort of pushing his beliefs on those kids who were not followers of his religion, but he wasn't doing it in a harmful way. Presumptuous, yes. Harmful, no. It's when Christians become so arrogant that their way *must* be your way, too—or they'll burn your sacred book—that harm is done.

Boy Scouts
and Other Options

So I guess you can tell from the title where I'm going with this one. My younger kid wanted to join the Scouts. He saw a recruitment poster in his school cafeteria. There were pictures of boys participating in outdoor activities, such as archery, camping, kayaking, and shooting BB guns. A boy's dream, right?

"Will I really get to do all those things?" my son asked the Scout leader when I took him to the sign-up.

"Yes," the man said, laughing, "but not all at once." So we signed my kid up, and I paid the $35 membership fee.

My son was excited about the first meeting. All the boys were his age. He didn't know any of them, so there was potential to make a lot of new friends. The kids did some good things in those first few meetings. They picked up trash in the park. They learned how to draw a map, give a short speech, and identify certain plants.

Then came an e-mail from the den leader. There was a God and Religion class that he wanted the boys to attend. I wrote him back.

"We're agnostics. Is this class required?" I didn't hear back for a few days. Then I received a phone call.

I wanted you to know something, the den leader told me. Boy Scouts is a religious organization. You have to believe in a God to be a member, and you have to pledge faith to your God, memorize a God-based creed, and take a class on religion.

He told me more. The Scouts had been sued about ten years before by an atheist family. The Boy Scouts refused to open their organization to this atheist boy. So the Scouts chose to become a private organization and forgo government subsidies and benefits in order to legally say "no" to those they want to exclude, like nonbelievers.

Of course, for my son, this was quite a blow. He either had to lie or quit. He really liked the Scouts; he loved playing with all the kids and running around outside. It was fun, and they did good deeds. I told my son that he could try out any religion he'd like, that we'd go together as a family to the church of his choosing.

My son struggled with this for a few days—he considered joining a church, trying to believe so that he could stay in Scouts. He had been trying to figure it all out anyway, what he believed about God and religion, and all this was going to do was give him a bad taste for religion. When he found out the camping trip he'd signed up for included a church service, he was really mad. "Why are they forcing me to believe?" he asked.

He had come to the crossroad of religion in an often-irrational society. Our predominantly Christian nation says you have to believe or you cannot play. You have to profess your faith in an imaginary God in order to be accepted, in order to be included. That is totally illogical. My son understood that he couldn't force himself to believe in God any more than I can convince you that there's a goblin under your chair.

So, regrettably, he quit the Scouts, though he still missed the meetings and asked me a couple of times, "Can't we try asking them again if I have to believe?"

OTHER OPTIONS FOR WOULD-BE BOY SCOUTS

Here's information on organizations that are similar to Boy Scouts but with no religious requirements:

Baden-Powell Service Association (BPSA):
Youth and adults, male and female.
www.bpsa-us.org

Navigators USA: For boys and girls. www.navigatorsusa.org

Adventure Scouts Coed: Fully nondiscriminatory program.
www.adventurescoutsusa.org

4-H:
For boys and girls. Teaches responsibility
and leadership. www.4-h.org

FAMILY

▪ AND ▪

FRIENDS

Coming Out to
Family and Friends

If you were raised in a religious household, coming out of the closet to your family and friends is not easy. In fact, it may be very uncomfortable. There are many people I've met through my blog who cannot envision being open about their beliefs. They have concerns like these: "Because I live in the South, I am extremely fearful to let my community know I am not a Christian. People here are so radical."

Or this: "I have an eight-year-old daughter, and I have often struggled with the fear of expressing my lack of belief in God. I've always been afraid kids in my daughter's school—or even the adults—would ridicule her. Or that neighbors, family, or friends would make life difficult for her because of my beliefs. Isn't it strange that we nonbelievers have to walk on eggshells around the subject of religion?"

Others are not so much fearful as they just want to avoid the harassment: "I work as a teacher in a neighboring district where my coworkers have no idea I am without religion. I am not brave enough to 'come out' to them. Even though I work in a public school, religion is very prevalent in the school and community. The nonbelievers are given a very hard time and I just don't want to deal with the constant pressure and invitations to visit their church."

Many of us who have come out have experienced varying degrees of acceptance. In my case, my parents were okay with it, but not everyone in my family was so accepting. My brother thought I was nothing short of an idiot for not believing. Faith is not grounded in logic, so it's hard to argue using logic; name-calling becomes an easy defense mechanism to fall back on. He said, "Listen, I pray and believe in God because those are the values that were instilled in me as a child. Do I believe in God? Absolutely. I don't think a fart blew apart a rock and my latest relative was a monkey." Always the joker, even in a serious conversation. But I understood that, for him and for other believers, the idea that you and I don't think God is or was real is a difficult concept to grasp. From the believer's vantage point, nonbelievers have no foundation or moral compass. What drives us to be good, to do the right thing? How do we explain the difficult questions in life: Why are we here? Where are we going?

Sometimes, though, we don't even need to bring up the topic of religion with our families. Belief is a personal preference, much like coffee or tea. This is not a cop-out; it's recognizing that revelation is not always required or important. When you're an adult, it's not necessary to share that you don't believe. At Thanksgiving, you can listen to your relatives talk and make mental notes that reinforce your decision not to believe in something that doesn't make sense to you and your kids. I know. I've been there. I also know that coming out makes people feel insecure. You're attacking the underpinnings of their morality, their hope, and their God. You're telling others, by your dissent, that their God is bogus, that their beliefs don't make sense. Unless you are in your own home, where we all should be free to believe or not to believe as we wish, making an issue of your lack of faith just makes everyone else feel uncomfortable.

As for my friends, some of them just think that I don't go to church, not that I don't believe in God. Why tell them anything different unless I have to? As humans, we always have private thoughts, things we keep to ourselves that we don't share with others. My personal views don't change the friend I am. However, if speaking up dissolves the friendship, then you know that person did not really accept you for who you are but for someone your friend wanted you to be.

I had to tell my family when, after years of blogging anonymously, I wrote a more public piece. My mom didn't say much about my revelation, but I felt her disappointment. I think she believed that, even though I didn't go to church anymore, I still, someplace in my head, believed in God. Even now, I think she hopes that I will come around and believe again, though she certainly understands the pitfalls of religion and the hypocrisy of the religious. My dad seemed to understand because he had been where I was before, and he still had his doubts. Or perhaps he just didn't care what my views were—live and let live. Once my family knew, however, it got easier with time, in accordance with the proverbial saying. Time really is a panacea. Besides, what were they going to do—disown me because I didn't believe that God was real? I'm sure some parents do, but of course, that says a lot about their own dysfunction and has nothing to do with your beliefs.

Sometimes you just can't avoid speaking out. There are ways we can come out gently, mainly by speaking kindly and being nonconfrontational. Marriage comes to mind: You and your partner want a civil ceremony, but your parents expected a church wedding. (If you're not a baptized Christian, you cannot have a sacramental marriage in the Catholic Church, even if your partner is a member in good standing.) You could offer this to parents, remembering that Mom and Dad may not agree, but they love you unconditionally: "I don't feel right being married in a church since my beliefs have changed, but I'll ask the Justice of the Peace to insert a few moments of silence into the ceremony so that you can pray for God's blessing." Or maybe you're visiting your parents during the holidays. You might tell them, "I don't celebrate Christmas as a religious holiday, but I'd be glad to accompany you to church. I just won't participate in the parts of the service that require belief, like communion."

Perhaps you've just had a baby, and your mom has already contacted the priest about the child's baptism. You might say: "I lost my faith along the way, but I am happy that you still find comfort in your beliefs. I'm not baptizing the baby, but she will be free to accept any religion she chooses when she's older."

I'll share a funny story. A woman I know was very anxious that her son, who was brought up Catholic, had agreed to bring their newborn up in his wife's Baptist church. Grandma was distressed that the child was not being baptized in the Catholic Church as an infant—actually would not be baptized for years. What if the child died? She believed that the baby would go to hell or remain indefinitely in purgatory, "in limbo." So the grandmother did a little research on the Internet, and the next time she babysat, she secretly took the infant into her bathroom and sprinkled water on his head, repeating the words that she had read would baptize the baby. A bathroom baptism, right there next to the toilet and the shower. Crazy, I know. Harmful? Of course not.

If you are aware that your mother or father desperately wants to baptize your child, you might consider saying this: "I appreciate that you did what you thought was right for me as a baby, but I prefer not to choose a religion for my child at this time. I will definitely let him choose when he gets old enough to decide for himself. And you are welcome to contribute your input when he is older." If in the end, you cave to baptism pressure, I wouldn't be too upset. You're just keeping the peace. Your kid will never remember a few sprinkles of water and a fancy outfit, and no harm has been done.

If, after opening up about your views, you are faced with offensive or hurtful remarks from family or friends, I'd suggest that we can stay true to ourselves without sacrificing what we believe simply by saying, "I respect your right to worship and believe. Please respect my right not to." Don't try to explain your reasons why; just dismiss the topic as quickly as possible. Remember that your loved ones get angry out of fear—fear of losing their own beliefs (there is strength in numbers), and out of fear that you will take the express train to hell rather than the elevator to heaven. They desire certainty and a happy ending. Don't we all?

When to Spill the Beans

O ur parents always used to say, "Don't talk religion or politics." There's nothing more divisive than those two topics. Yet sometimes, we *need* to talk about our religious beliefs. Coming out to friends and family can be difficult for many reasons, and each situation, each person, is different. In determining whether or not to spill the beans, ask yourself the following questions.

A. Is keeping quiet and playing along causing you grief?

If yes, go to question 2. If no, keep reading here: Sometimes, it's easier to just play along. I'll give you an example. My eighty-something-year-old grandmother was a devout Catholic, and she believed with every last cell in her body that she would meet her entire family in heaven. She was a simple woman, and her family was her world. Why hurt her by telling her I'm not a believer? She would only worry about me, and she did not have the ability to even begin to understand why I'm a nonbeliever. We were from different generations, different worlds, and to even broach the topic would be heretical.

B. Do you know this person?

If yes, go on to question 3. If no, keep reading here: If you don't know the person, and you've been cornered in some place (or even at your home) by Jesus salespeople, then, by all means, share your views with them. This doesn't mean you have to steamroll them with science or with contradictions from their own Bible. Just say, "No, thanks, I don't believe, and I prefer not to discuss this with you." However, if you are up for a little entertainment and would like a reminder of why you're not a believer, you may find yourself wanting to engage in a conversation with God's headhunters. But always, since we represent "our kind," I think we should avoid being belligerent or hostile. It only turns us into one of them. (Think of all the antagonistic evangelicals you know.) We want to be the voice of reason, and that means leaving emotion out of our conversations. I know, I know. Sometimes people can be frustrating. You and I realize that the very annoying strangers trying to sell us on their God or their church don't even realize they are *not* working for God, but for themselves. Finding converts helps them get to heaven, and all they're trying to do is save themselves. Still, we have to forgive them for their ignorance.

C. Are you friends or family?

If you are family, go on to question 4. If you are friends, read here: Friendships are like marriages. You and your friend are attracted to each other for some reason, and you have to be compatible to sustain the relationship. There is some commonality to which you can relate. Sometimes, these common interests change. Sometimes, we just outgrow our friends. But I can tell you that, while you may mourn the loss of a friend because of religious differences, if your friend is offended by your lack of beliefs, ultimately, you're better off. Trust me, in most cases, those types of friends won't respect your views. Mainstream religions teach their followers that their way is the right and only way, so naturally your friends will always be right. And if you come clean that you're a nonbeliever, you'll always be a threat to and a splinter in their "spirit" (or psyche, to us). Why a threat? Because you reject their belief system, and in doing so, you tell them their beliefs don't make sense. Because, when it comes to religion, there is strength in numbers. And when you doubt, when you say you don't believe, you make them feel insecure about their own beliefs. Nonbelievers like you and me will always look askance at our religious friends and wonder how flipping crazy is it to believe that God is talking to them or has planned out the minutiae of their lives. Every time we hear a "Godism," we'll cringe. And every time we hear a Christian friend complain about giving access to affordable health care to the poor, we'll note the hypocrisy because Jesus enthusiasts are supposed to love their neighbors and help the less fortunate.

On the other hand, there will be some friends you can come out to without jeopardizing your friendship. You'll know who they are: friends who are loosely tethered to their religions or friends who are just more tolerant in general. To these friends, your disclosure will mean nothing more than a preference for a certain color or a certain beer or wine.

D. **If you cannot stand it any more,** and need to be heard and understood by your family, you might just softly say (and I've had to do this), "I'm sorry. I've given my religious belief a lot of thought and consideration. I respect how you believe, [Mom, Dad, Brother, etc.], but I just don't believe any more. I'm agnostic/atheist."

While my mom is, like any other mother, devoted and loving, I think it does pain her that I don't believe. After I die, I won't be going wherever she is. There is a chasm, too, when we talk, because she believes in things like mediums and spirits, and she knows I don't.

I understand her need for these things, and I listen to her and don't criticize. We have to consider the intentions of the people who love us. I know my mother is disappointed in me, and I realize that coming out to her was better for me, but clearly not for her. She prays for me because she doesn't want me going to the deep, deep South after I die. That's fine. Her prayers don't hurt me, but they bring her some kind of comfort. From my perspective, it was better to be honest than to continue living a lie—or worse, to have my mom find out from someone else who had read my articles. Yes, I will still attend church with her, but I will not participate as a believer, only as a person who respects others' traditions. I sit and stand on cue, but I do not say the prayers or take the sacraments.

Sometimes, you might encounter some anger or resistance, rather than sadness and disappointment. Again, I suggest that we just calmly continue to tell others, "I respect your right to believe. Please respect my right not to." We will not gain acceptance by kicking down the front door. We have to desensitize believers and let them know we are not a threat to them. No matter what we say, they will not budge from their place of belief or understand where we are coming from. We cannot open a door for them. They will have to do it themselves. The best we can hope for is that they leave us in peace. American Christians are like no other. Some believe they have an inalienable right to force their belief system on everyone else, whether it's an individual, a group of people, or a nation, and our goal is to break free from that mind-set.

There is a tolerance paradox, meaning we are sometimes intolerant of those who are not tolerant and hence intolerant ourselves. I know I can fall into this trap, but I try to remember where intolerance comes from. It grows out of fear and out of focusing too much on the self, and those are two things that religion encourages. A lot.

In all interactions with those who believe, whether the person is our best friend or a stranger, I think we should be good representatives for our cause and show them that we are not waging war on religion; we just want the same rights and respect as believers. We don't try to talk them out of believing, and we don't want the religious to try to talk us into believing. We are not in the market for God or religion. Should we offer unconditional tolerance? Of course not. We know when people are dangerous or are overstepping their boundaries, and we have a right to assert ourselves and a duty to protect our children.

Leaving

When my grandmother's life was winding down, the undignified way in which she was dying just seemed to further suggest the existential nature of our lives. We're born alone, we exist without knowing why, and we die alone. A complete circle—helplessness to helplessness. We are imperfect, prone to illnesses, accidents, and breakdowns, and yet we are perfectly in sync with nature. We are fugacious like flowers; our bodies rise and set like the sun; we have seasons; we spread our seeds; and we age like trees.

But there is no grace in dying from disease or from old age. The mind struggles to remember, to hang on. Knuckles become gnarled. The teeth and eyes yellow. The skin collapses in on itself. Everything hangs. The body starts shutting down. Eventually it begins to smell of death.

The process of dying seems very natural, yes. But there's no sign of a loving God when you see how unmercifully people die. You'd think that a woman who said her rosary every day, who was always thankful, who always lived the life of a good Catholic—you'd think that woman, at least, would be spared a humiliating, painful end, bleeding to death from stomach cancer. If there is a God, he leaves people very lonely in their time of greatest need. That is not love.

My grandmother was one of the most beautiful women I've ever known. She was the counterbalance to evil. You could see kindness in her light blue eyes, hear gentleness in her voice. When we visited her, she cooked us every meal and gave up her own bed so we could be comfortable. She was an incredibly robust woman, with limitless patience and love for her family. She taught me so many sayings of "the old timers." "Those old timers," she'd say in her sharp Jersey accent, "they knew what they were talking about. You'd think they wouldn't know anything because they weren't educated, but they did. They were smarter that you realize." Yes, Grandma, I'd say. I know they were smart. And I meant it.

She walked that fine line between preaching and giving advice. "If you love your children, you won't spoil them," she'd tell me over and over. Truly, I've raised my children by that one. And when I compared my kids to each other, my grandmother would say, "You know, Deb, if all the birds ate the same seed, it would be a boring world."

When I last saw her, save for a few lucid moments, she could remember nothing. It's as if a tornado had run through her brain and thrown pieces of her memory everywhere—total chaos. She could not remember where she lived, if her parents were alive and how old she was. She didn't know she had three daughters. She confused names, dates, and places. Her face puffed up like a caricature of her younger self. But, still, that gentleness in her voice was there.

It seemed so damn inhumane to let her suffer, and I knew she would not want to live like that. We treat our animals better. It's too bad there's not a button we can push when we're ready to go—so that we don't have live through all the pain and humiliation of a body and mind that's unraveling.

If I don't die in a fiery crash or in my sleep, if I have a prolonged and painful illness, I'd want a loving family member to put me out of my misery with an end-of-life cocktail. I don't want to make my loved ones watch me fall apart. I don't want them to be burdened with caring for someone who has lived past her usefulness—and who is just wasting precious resources. I don't want to taint their memories of me.

No matter how happily we lived, no matter what kind words we said, those few ugly moments at the end can lodge inextricably in the brains of those who loved us.

Dealing with Death
in the Family

As nonbelievers, how do we help the people we love when they are dying? I know, we are all dying, but when death is close, how do we give comfort?

My father died this past summer. He was a healthy guy, and for six months his doctor gave him steroid shots in his back, thinking that all the running, weight lifting, and tennis had hurt him. It turns out that he had pancreatic cancer. Once he was diagnosed, he died in less than two months. I flew down to spend two out of his last four weeks with him. It was a difficult thing to see—a strong man struggling with the inevitability and nearness of his death, yet clinging to the hope of just one more year of life, which his doctor said might be possible.

After he died, people who knew him said the expected niceties: He didn't suffer long. At least you had time to get to know him. He's in God's hands. He's in a better place now.

That last comment is the one that brings me to tears, even now. My father loved this place, this planet, with all its flaws and unpredictability. He had a huge appetite for learning and reading and thinking. He never talked about heaven because, well, what could be better than this? But what I saw as his biggest fear when he was dying was that he would make the journey from life to death alone. I think now that must be the closest we get to hell—the lonely movement from this life into nothingness and the fear you feel knowing that you're about to be gone forever.

Towards the end, he had Sundown Syndrome. He would grow agitated in the evening as it started to get dark in the house, so in the late afternoon my mother would rush around turning on all the lights in the house to simulate daytime. But, somehow, the body knows. And Sundown Syndrome must surely be a way that the body recognizes, consciously or not, that it's near the end of its own day. My dad knew, intuitively, that his life was wrapping up, even though he was fighting hard to stay alive—as he said—for just one more year.

How do we comfort the dying? My friend's mom was comforted by the fact that her God was going to meet her after she took her last breath. Her death was not nearly as much of a struggle. We nonbelievers don't have the luxury of that fantasy. It's not even something that we can pretend to believe. For those of us who don't believe, we just have to hold tight to each other. For the first time in his life, my father reached his hand out to me—and I held it. That way of making a connection was not only a bridge to another person, but also an offer of forgiveness for all the hurt, for all the things we wished we had said but didn't. At the end of the day, he just wanted me to know he loved me. That's all any of us really need to know from our parents. He talked and talked and talked, more than I'd ever heard him, perhaps just to make sure he was still part of this world or perhaps because he wanted to express all he meant to put into words over the years.

He was bothered by two things. The first was that he was leaving my mother behind, and he asked her, *Please, go with me. We can empty this morphine bottle together.* My mom had never dated anyone else, and she married him at nineteen years of age. They were one of those couples who loved each other so much they were sort of oblivious to everyone and everything else. His pain at leaving her behind to fend for herself, which seemed as bad as his fear of dying, was touching. In the weeks before he died, concerned that she would be on her own, he frantically wrote out all instructions for her on anything he had taken care of as her husband.

The second was that he felt as if he had been a bad parent. And the funny thing is, to me, he was just the typical, hardworking, distant father of his generation. He was a great father and a great man, I told him, and I believed it, knowing that you can only judge people by what *they* are capable of—not by what anyone else wants them to be. To me, he was always more of a peer, but that was fine. There was always my mother setting us straight and giving us unconditional love. My father and I talked a lot about articles or books we'd read, both having strong interests in math and science (yes, I nearly failed freshman English). I called him for investment advice and, over the last few years, he sometimes called me.

In the end, my dad was placed into hospice, and when my mother left one night to go home and shower, my father, who had a deep-rooted fear of anything that smacked of a hospital, got up from his bed and wandered the halls, looking for her. He was panicked and thrashing about. The nurses subdued him, and medicated him so that he never woke up again. Having had other family members with terminal illnesses, I know this much: People are sometimes put down just like horses and dogs.

For the next few days, he slept deeply until, with my mom present, he took his last breath and quietly died. Humanely, with lots of medications.

TRISH'S STORY: LOSS AND EMPTY WORDS

When Trish, who lives in Texas, lost her daughter, those around her did not offer help, but they offered prayers. Prayers, of course, didn't help her feel better; they didn't help with the day-to-day struggles of living after the death of a child. She shares her experience of loss, grief, and disappointment:

I was raised Catholic, but never really "got it" or got into it. I didn't get the guilt factor. At first I thought there was a God, as I had been told, but I didn't get why we had to tell a priest our "sins" when this God was supposed to know everything anyway (and such terrible things I did at age ten).

After I was married and began trying to start a family, my husband and I found out we had fertility issues. I was told by "Christian" friends that my husband's infertility was "God's way of bringing you to your knees to Christ."

I heard the typical statements: "Pray more," "God works in mysterious ways," and "We aren't supposed to question God." And the more people told me about their God, it made me think that this God sounds more like a Deadbeat Dad than a loving, caring father. In fact, if any "real-life" person treated us the way God treats people, we wouldn't be his friend.

We did get pregnant with twins sixteen years ago, and religious people told me that my children were not "real" humans because they were created through IVF. When one of my twin daughters died at eight months old, I was told that "God needed her more," and that there was a reason he took her—a reason I wasn't supposed to understand. We had to remove her from life support and as I sat there holding her dying body (my last moments with her), the hospital chaplain came in and starting yapping about his God. My last moments were ruined by someone so obsessed with his idol that he couldn't even tell that it was a bad time to blab about being God's greatest fan.

When my living daughter was diagnosed with a disability, I was told once again, that God had a reason. I shouldn't question it. When my younger brother died a few years after that, we were told that God put him here on earth for a short time and that God works in mysterious ways. Blah, blah, blah. (You get the idea; you've heard it.) When my dad died the next year, my mom was told that she "didn't pray hard enough, and at the right level." (That one is my favorite.)

I have heard these types of comments in hundreds of different forms, from hundreds of people, all claiming to be good Christians. And when I mention these terrible comments to Christians, they are quick to say, "Oh, those people are wrong; that's not how a true Christian acts." But they all say it about each other.

My opinion is that the God presented to me (by his followers) is nothing that I would ever worship, love, or respect.

I hear many people talking about what a good Christian is and I have to laugh. I think that, as an atheist, I am a better Christian than most Christians. I think I am kinder and more giving—donating, helping strangers, bringing meals, supporting causes, letting people in line ahead of me—that kind of stuff. As my thirteen-year-old son said in regard to people who live here in Texas, "Most people are trying so hard to look like a good Christian that none of them know how to act like one." They quote the Bible and wear the crosses and go to church, but not a single one of them offered help when my daughter was in the hospital. Oh, wait. They did offer to pray for us.

I can't imagine that if I get to heaven and find out there is a God, he/she is going to look at me, at the good I've done, at the children I've raised, and say (in a most immature middle school voice), "But, YOU didn't like ME, so you can't stay here."

Ways to Help the Dying

The best gift we can give—actually to anyone, living or dying—is our time and our kindness. When a person we love is dying, we realize how little material things really mean: We realize that our time and spending it with the people we love is more important than our jobs, than anything we can put on, than anything we can drive. I remember how touched my dad was that so many people stopped by just to talk with him and just to let him know that they were thinking of him.

When a loved one is dying from a terminal illness, we can give her comfort by offering her immortality through videotapes or through the written word. Offer to tape her as she says her good-byes, or ask her to tell stories from her past that she wants to pass on to future generations. I did this with my grandmother, who had the most amazing stories to tell about her childhood and about the Great Depression. My grandmother wrote out answers to questions I had asked her. Later, after she died, I posted her responses on a blog to share with family, where they could also add their own memories.

You can also write letters on loved ones' behalf. Maybe there's an apology or peace that needs to be made. Maybe there's wisdom to share or a good memory that needs to be preserved. Tell your loved ones how they've impacted your life and what that means to you. What memories will you carry? Remind them of the legacy they leave behind: children or grandchildren, a company they started, a contribution they made to their employer or their community, donations that helped someone in need. Let your loved ones know that they will continue to live on in other ways.

Tell them how you will ask others to honor them or ask how they want to be honored. For my dad, my mom set up a scholarship fund at his alma mater. In lieu of flowers, donations went toward providing scholarships for engineering students.

Help your loved one tie up loose ends. Is there anything a spouse or child will need to know to help make the transition after death easier? My father wrote step-by-step instructions for my mom on how to troubleshoot any problems with the Internet or television. He told her exactly what would need to be shut off in the house if she went away on a trip. You might help type these letters up or make phone calls so that the dying know that their spouses or children will not be burdened with so many details when they are grieving. In this way, the dying can also feel better knowing that they have cared for their loved ones, even after death.

With families spread out across the country, sometimes we can't be with the person who is dying, or we can't be with him as much as he wants. Make a tape or a video—from you, your siblings, or your children—telling your loved one how much he means to you. That tape or video can be played when you're not there. There is always Skype, which allows you to see and talk with family for free via your phone, computer, or television.

Make a photo book. My dad got a lot of enjoyment from photo albums. When we found out he was dying—and would die soon—I made an album of the fiftieth-wedding anniversary he and my mom had just celebrated. The happiness of having all the people he loved gathered together was palpable. I included some words he had written for the vow-renewal ceremony. I think it gave him a lot of pleasure to know his thoughts were permanently in a book that my mom could pick up and read at any time. At the end of this essay, I've shared a touching letter he wrote for my mother because his sentiments will resonate with many couples.

Perhaps one of the most important things we can do, whether those who are dying believe in God and an afterlife or they believe that this life is it, is just be accepting. If they believe in an afterlife, they might ask you if you share their beliefs. Most likely, they just want reassurance that there's a chance you will all meet again. Agreement helps bring credibility to ideas, even though, as you and I know, no matter how many people think heaven exists, the likelihood that there is something more after this life is very, very slim. Regardless, never underestimate the power of a smile and a nod or the squeeze of hand. It does not mean you are compromising your beliefs; rather, it is a form of giving—without even saying a word. Another person's peace costs us nothing.

I'd also like to share a story that another parent told me. We often hear stories about people who die and are brought back to life. They see a "bright light" and are greeted by people they love. Nonbelievers like us roll our eyes and wonder why all those stories sound suspiciously similar. One atheist mother, Carrie, shared an experience she had with dying after surgery: "I have accepted that when I die, that is it. I actually already 'died' three years ago after a surgery, and there was nothing, zero, zip. And having already died, I am less scared than ever. It was a total absence of everything, and that included pain and suffering. Even in a deep sleep, there is some consciousness that you are alive. But this was utter nothingness. It is nothing to fear, therefore I don't."

MY FATHER'S WORDS

Over the fifty years we have been married and the three years we were together prior to our wedding, you have been 125 percent supportive and always met me more than halfway as we moved through this fifty-three-year sojourn.

Simply put, you are my love, my lover, my friend, my business partner, my confidant, and my reason to look forward to an even older age.

Words that I plucked out of my mind fifty years ago when I was mad and wild with love still hold true now, however tempered with the weight of age. What makes my love go on? Desire, desire, desire. Desire: the eternal longing for the connection that will be maintained across years and through our respective lifetimes and beyond. As we feel the wind blow both harder and colder and the palms rub against our windowpanes and the beams in our house creak, my Darling, will you remember the man you married? Touch me often and remind me that you do.

—Tom Mitchell, June 2013

Eulogy from a Physicist

aron Freeman is a writer and performer, living in Chicago. He wrote this beautiful piece, called "Eulogy from a Physicist." I asked him if he believes in God, and he responded, "I believe in Nike, goddess of victory; Anapurna, goddess of food; Sophia, of wisdom; Shango, of the sky; and absolutely in Dionysus, of wine making and theater!" Whether you are a believer or a nonbeliever, these moving words unite us all:

> *You want a physicist to speak at your funeral. You want the physicist to talk to your grieving family about the conservation of energy, so they will understand that your energy has not died. You want the physicist to remind your sobbing mother about the first law of thermodynamics; that no energy gets created in the universe, and none is destroyed. You want your mother to know that all your energy, every vibration, every Btu of heat, every wave of every particle that was her beloved child remains with her*

in this world. You want the physicist to tell your weeping father that amid energies of the cosmos, you gave as good as you got.

And at one point you'd hope that the physicist would step down from the pulpit and walk to your brokenhearted spouse there in the pew and tell him that all the photons that ever bounced off your face, all the particles whose paths were interrupted by your smile, by the touch of your hair, hundreds of trillions of particles, have raced off like children, their ways forever changed by you. And as your widow rocks in the arms of a loving family, may the physicist let her know that all the photons that bounced from you were gathered in the particle detectors that are her eyes, that those photons created within her constellations of electromagnetically charged neurons whose energy will go on forever.

And the physicist will remind the congregation of how much of all our energy is given off as heat. There may be a few fanning themselves with their programs as he says it. And he will tell them that the warmth that flowed through you in life is still here, still part of all that we are, even as we who mourn continue the heat of our own lives.

And you'll want the physicist to explain to those who loved you that they need not have faith; indeed, they should not have faith. Let them know that they can measure, that scientists have measured precisely the conservation of energy and found it accurate, verifiable, and consistent across space and time. You can hope your family will examine the evidence and satisfy themselves that the science is sound and that they'll be comforted to know your energy's still around. According to the law of the conservation of energy, not a bit of you is gone; you're just less orderly. Amen.

Instead of "I'll Pray for You"

'm sometimes in the awkward position of having friends or acquaintances ask me to pray for them. If they are asking me for prayers, they're probably distraught over something: a serious illness or an accident or an impending operation. At times, people will ask for prayers for an important event, such as an interview. Obviously, that's not the time to say, "I don't believe in prayer." Who would be so cruel, right? Yet it may be difficult to think of a few reassuring words to say without lying that you will pray. Sometimes, it's so much easier just to answer, "Okay." But we also want to teach our children that, while we must always strive to be kind, we should also be true to ourselves. Anything less than that will make us feel bad—and if the person requesting prayers finds out we're pretending—she will feel bad, too.

In responding to prayer requests, people usually won't even pick up on the fact that you've kept the word *prayer* out of your response. They just want to know that others are there for moral support. Here are a few go-to phrases that I use:

My thoughts are with you and your family.

Please know that I'll be thinking of you during your surgery [for example].

I'm sorry. Can I help by_____? [Fill in the blank with a specific action, such as picking up your daughter from school.]

I'm sorry you're in such pain. Please call any time you want to talk.

I have great memories of your brother. [Share a specific memory.]

I'm hoping for the very best outcome in your son's college interview.

If you are providing support to people who are grieving or suffering from trauma, just listen and offer them comfort and help, as needed. The last thing they need or want is advice on how to cope or what to do next. Sometimes a simple "I'm sorry" is best. Or "I'm sorry you're going through this. It must be really difficult." Don't share your stories, which might only cause more suffering, or turn the attention to you by saying how upset you are or how bad you feel. The fewer words the better; just be present and listen. No one will even realize you've left God out of the conversation.

Disapproving Grandparents

Should you tell your parents to butt out? That's a question that has come up a few times on my blog. Some people, when they see grandparenthood on the horizon, become exceedingly excited about the spiritual saving and recruitment of the young one's soul.

A mom from Mississippi shared her struggles:

> *My mother tells me that she does not have to respect my right not to believe because I don't have any beliefs. She tells my daughter that my husband and I are going to hell because we are atheists. I have told my mother that it is not her business to discuss religion with our daughter and if she has questions, they should be directed to us as her parents. It is a difficult thing when you are the only one in your family who doesn't believe.*

If your child ever spends the night away from you with his grandparents, that can be frustrating, too. You don't know what's going on while your child is in Grandma's or Grandpa's care. One parent wrote this:

My mother-in-law insists that my son attend church with her when he spends the night. He comes home from her house saying things like, "It's raining because someone made God cry." We don't mind him being exposed to different religions, but we don't want anyone, especially a family member who our son will trust, pushing religion on him. It's very frustrating.

Fortunately for me, my parents didn't try to intervene in how I raised my kids. But if they had been like some of the grandparents I've seen and heard of, planning a baptism and buying *Veggie Tales* while junior is still kicking his way around in the womb, then, at least at first, I would gently and softly say that religion is an important part of a child's education, but it should be offered later in life, like beer or wine, when the child is old enough to handle it. You, as the parent, are the judge of when that will be. Maybe your child will be curious and open the door for dialogue at age four or at age six or maybe not until the age of sixteen.

If your parents don't understand that you're asking them to check their religious agenda at the door, then you'll have to be more forceful, reminding them that they had a chance to raise and indoctrinate you as they believed appropriate, and now you'd like their trust and confidence in your abilities to raise and, yes, even indoctrinate, your own kids. The problem is, when children are young, they'll believe literally anything. (Hello, Easter Bunny.) And it's your job as a parent to pick and choose what to feed your child's body and brain.

Tell your family this because, if they want to be part of your child's life, they should respect your wishes. Explain that you don't want to hide, and that you don't want to be put in the position of secretly "deprogramming" your kid after they are gone. That doesn't send a good message about you, your beliefs, and how to interact with others.

Kids should learn about Christianity—when they are ready—and about every other worldview. Maybe you can tell your parents that, when your children are a little older, it will be okay for them to share their beliefs with your kids, but they should know that you're also going to teach that Christianity is just one of the *many* things people (not Mom and Dad) believe all over the world and throughout history. On the other hand, I also want to suggest that you take each situation on a case-by-case basis. If it causes your mother great grief, results in her having heart palpitations, to know her first (and perhaps only) grandchild will not be "saved" or purified right out of the shoot, you can compromise with a baptism. As I mentioned earlier, a child won't remember being dressed up in infant finery and displayed in front of an adoring congregation. It's okay. The whole thing will be painless, over before you know it, punctuated with a good meal and a few handshakes. Perhaps offer this: I'll baptize baby *only* if you (Grandparents A and B) will keep God in your heart and mind for the next eighteen years. If you don't allow God to cross your lips, if you don't preach about JC, then we have a deal. That will be very hard to negotiate, but a grandchild's salvation just might be worth it.

Request for Advice:
When Kids Are a Little Older

Grandparents play such a big role in our children's lives, and they have so much to offer: love, patience, time on the floor playing with dolls or Legos. I get a lot of questions about how to deal with Grandma or Grandpa or both, so I thought I'd include the following letter and my response. There are no easy answers when it comes to dealing with the people we love, but perhaps you can find one or two ideas that you can excerpt for your particular situation:

Good Afternoon,

I am a married thirty-five-year-old father of an eight-year-old girl and a three-year-old boy. I am among the readers who came to your blog after your CNN article was publicized. If you have the time, I would truly appreciate your advice on a matter that I feel you have great insight into.

I was raised in the Presbyterian Church but stopped attending church in my late teens. I began identifying myself as an atheist in my early twenties. My wife and I are on the same page about religion and child rearing. The problem lies with my side of the family. To the same degree that I have moved away from religion, my family, especially my mother and stepfather, have delved all the more deeply into religion, deciding to make the switch to what I refer to as "radicalized evangelicalism." If my mother has a spare dollar, she will send it off to an organization translating Bibles for Malaysia as opposed to remodeling her 1980s-era kitchen. Religion is not a part of my mother's life; religion is her life. She and my stepfather work only enough to support a baseline of middle class existence, devoting most of their financial resources and time to evangelism.

The problem lies in my mother's role as a grandmother to my children. By all accounts, my mother is an excellent grandmother. She is always there for my kids, whether that be by Skype, or phone, or frequent visit. My mother, however, cannot separate being a grandmother to my children from being their spiritual mentor. After every interaction she has with my kids (that I am not present for), my kids return to me chock-full of religious nonsense. I find my daughter illustrating stories involving Jesus, asking me to take her to a local church, and requesting to pray before meals. I feel as though I need to "shake the Jesus" out of my kids at the door whenever I get them back.

I have frequently asked my mother to just be a grandmother, and respect my wishes that she not speak to my kids about her religion. I have tried using every logical device I can think of to communicate my point of view to my mother, with no success. I understand this is largely because, as a devout evangelical, reason and logic are dirty words and tools of the Devil to be avoided. This divide between my mother and me has come to a head as my daughter is now old enough to fly several states away to stay with my mother for a two-week period. My daughter is already ecstatic about this trip, and my wife and I are dreading it. We know we will have a solid couple of months of kid-size evangelism coming back to us. We know that my mother will insist on taking our daughter to Sunday school, and ensure she prays before every meal, before bed, and will be asked to commit her eight-year-old soul to Christ.

Do I play hardball with my Mom and make ultimatums about never allowing her unsupervised time with my daughter? It seems when I describe the situation to others, there is largely an attitude that I am making too big a deal out of this. Am I overreacting? Am I being unrealistic to think I should be able to filter out the religion aimed at my children's impressionable minds? I also feel that if I take a hard-line approach of limiting interaction between my children and my mother, I will turn out to be the bad guy in my children's eyes. My kids could "rebel" against their old man by signing up for Vacation Bible School.

I am sorry for the length of this e-mail, and truly appreciate any advice you are willing to provide.

Sincerely,

Concerned Dad

Here is my reply:

Dear Concerned Dad,

First, I want you to know that you are not alone. There are many others in similar situations. It's really good that you and your wife are on the same page. That makes things easier.

I can tell that you love your mom, but you also want to do the right thing for your daughter (and son). There is nothing better than a loving grandmother, and the fact that your daughter is so excited about visiting her says a lot. And you're right— you would be forever burned in your daughter's memory as the bad guy for keeping her from a doting grandmother.

On the other hand, you are not being unrealistic in any way in asking your mother to cease and desist. You should tell your mom that you love her very much. She's been a great mother and grandmother, and you appreciate that she is concerned about your daughter. But she's had a chance to raise you as she saw fit, and you would like the chance to do the same with your children. Tell her that this is so important to you that you will limit the time she has with your children to only the times when you can supervise. I know you've told her something along these lines already, but it's worth one more try.

The key part is this. Tell your daughter you have something important to talk to her about. Go for a walk or take her for a hot chocolate so that she feels this is a serious and special moment. (It is.) I would then tell your daughter that, just as many kids believe in Santa, the Easter Bunny, ghosts in their closets, and monsters under their bed, some adults grow up and believe in similar stories. These are myths, just stories, and guesses about how we got here. (Keep it simple.) Tell her that Mom and Dad don't believe these things, but Grandmom grew up in a different generation, and she believes that. Then you can have the "Does this make sense?" talk with your daughter. (I did this with my kids—several times.) You ask her things like this: "Some people believe that there is a man in the sky that can see and hear everyone on the planet at the same time. Does this make sense to you?" Ask her if she knows anyone who can do that. You can ask a few other questions along these lines. "Some people think that when it's raining, God made that happen or that God is crying. Do you know how we get rain? When the sun comes out and heats water on the planet, that causes moisture to rise (just like the moisture you see from the stove when you heat water)." You get the idea. There are many examples you could use to show her that the stories she's hearing don't make sense. People (young and old) like to scare kids with stories about Satan, so talk to her about the Devil, too. "Does it make sense that there's a Devil under the ground who will reach up and grab your feet? What happens when you dig in the dirt? Do you see anyone?" Tell her that Satan is a word jumble for Santa, and they're both not real. Since kids are easily spooked, you will desensitize her by asking her lots of questions and letting her figure things out for herself.

Remind your daughter that even though you don't agree with Grandma, you still love and respect her. You don't try to talk her out of her beliefs. You just don't believe the same things as she does. Grandma should also respect how everyone else *believes. Your daughter will encounter all sorts of believers along her journey throughout life. I think if you help her reason things out now, that will absolutely be your best weapon. You might even tell your daughter that you, too, used to believe in God when you were little because everyone told you to, but then you grew up and started thinking about things, and all these stories didn't make sense. No matter what Grandma tells you now, you will never believe that way again. Just as you will not believe in things like the Easter Bunny and ghosts.*

And one more thing—tell your daughter, if she gets confused at any time while she's at Grandma's, that she can call you or Mom.

Now, when your daughter visits Grandma, it is only fair that Grandma be allowed to pray in her own home. I told my kids that when we are at the homes of people who pray, we participate in prayers by bowing our heads to show respect, but we don't say anything. I also had to tell my boys not to talk about religion at all with their great-grandmother. I just told them she was older and doesn't understand how we think. It's okay. They could just listen to her. She's just telling stories of who she thinks made the world and how we got here.

Good luck. Please let me know how it goes.

Kind regards,
Deborah Mitchell

The Best Thing We
Can Give to Our Kids

Our kids know. Yours do; mine do. They know what kind of relationship we have with our spouses. We can't fake it.

This is a point that both religious and nonreligious couples can agree on: A good marriage or partnership is crucial for raising emotionally healthy kids.

An attorney friend of mine once said that the biggest cause of divorce was that our ideal doesn't match our reality. We live in two worlds at once: the ideal, which is held privately inside our minds, and the real, which is our messy day-to-day life. Someplace inside our heads is a vision of what a marriage should look like, what love should feel and sound like. But swirling around our physical existence is what's real.

We see this at Christmastime. Everyone wants to experience the Currier & Ives version of the holidays: hot chocolate, good cheer, gift giving, caroling, kissing under the mistletoe, and festive holiday parties. But, often, the reality is long lines at the store, grumpy drivers, sloppy-drunk coworkers, gifts that disappoint, kids who misbehave, credit card bills that won't be paid off for decades, and soul-sucking materialism.

Yet in spite of all that, in between what we envision and what's real, there are the sweet voices of our children, smiles from strangers, random acts of kindness, donations to food pantries, and gifts to needy children. And at the end of the day, we can still love our fellow man because, even though he stole our parking space at Costco, he still held the door open for us when our hands were full. Most people do good things most of the time. There is hope for humanity because, overall, people do *try* to keep improving. There is still a human desire to make the world a better place.

How does all this relate to our marriages? We can be aware of the ideals, the fantasies, the fairy tales that we hang onto through childhood and into adulthood. We can change our perception and notice what is good in our spouses and in our marriages. The best gift we can give to our kids is a quality relationship with the other parent whether we are married or divorced. We can give this any day, every day. It's never too late, no matter how much we have stumbled, no matter how many fights we've already had. The ability to adapt and change is one of nature's greatest gifts to us, and it is a key component of happiness. I know a lot of unhappy couples. We only get one chance to live on this planet, and we don't want to spend our days—not even one of them—unhappy because we don't feel loved. Unhappy people infect others, especially their kids, who then grow up and infect their kids.

Familiarity does tend to breed the proverbial contempt. But living with someone day in and day out doesn't mean you have to think of him as an old boot. (Someone I know really referred to her husband this way.) You can think of him as your co-conspirator, as the person for whom you abandoned the single life in favor of traveling life's roads together. It takes a bit of attitude adjustment: You have to look past the strident burps and the globs of toothpaste in the sink. Every day, you have to recognize and be thankful for the nice things your spouse does, no matter how small, and you have to let go of things that annoy you (most likely he didn't annoy you when you were trying to win his affection). This takes a bit of work, more so for some than for others.

It's worth the work—for yourself and your kids—to stay together if you have anything salvageable in your relationship. Having gone through a divorce, I know that it is an emotionally and physically wrenching experience. This is why I've told several of my unhappily wed girlfriends, "If your husband wants to work things out and you guys are compatible, if he can talk to you about how he feels, then you should try. Try, try, try." (Same goes for wives.) People change and marriages change. They age; they ripen. If they are bad, they can become good again. If they are mediocre, they can become excellent. A couple can have whatever they both want. If both want a good marriage or a solid union, they will have that. If only one wants a good marriage, and the other spouse is looking for a way out, then the relationship is doomed.

Our children are watching, and they know more than we realize.

Parents and Marriages
of Different Faiths

What do you do when you and your partner have different beliefs about God? I grew up in such a family, with one parent who was a devout Catholic and the other who did not identify with any religion. They agreed before getting married that their children would be brought up Catholic until we were old enough to choose for ourselves. That worked for them.

So I was baptized at just a few weeks of age, cleansed of the naughtiness I was born with, thanks to Eve's thirst for knowledge, and brought into the church before I could even say no or ask why. And then I received my First Holy Communion and was allowed to eat the body of Christ. Fortunately for my mother, I didn't learn about transubstantiation until I went to college because I never would have willingly eaten the body of Christ. And if I did learn about transubstantiation in the Confraternity of Christian Doctrine (CCD), I was probably checked out, as usual, staring out the window, thinking of what I'd do once I was set free that Saturday morning. I was later confirmed, before I hit my teen years, as an adult member of the Roman Catholic Church.

My mother took us faithfully every Sunday, no matter how much snow we had to dig through, no matter how busy we were. My father, on the other hand, sat in his recliner and read the newspaper while we worshipped, save for two days: Christmas and Easter. Those were the two days he had agreed to accompany my mother to church.

Of course, I used to complain that I should be allowed to stay home "like Dad," and I remember asking him one day, when I was around eight years old, why he didn't go to church with us. I am grateful that he was honest, not just because it was the right thing to do but because I would respect him more for telling me he stood apart, yet supported my mother. He told me he wasn't Catholic but had agreed that my brother and I would be raised as members of the church. It's a great act of love to set aside your own personal feelings to support your spouse in doing what she thinks is best.

But marriages are not always this harmonious when it comes to faith. In a recently published *New York Times* article, titled "Interfaith Unions: A Mixed Blessing," author Naomi Schaefer Riley found that, what is good for society is not always good for couples.[4] While families of mixed faith helped create a culture of tolerance, Riley found in her research that some combinations of religions make for unhappy interfaith marriages and are more likely to lead to divorce.

This was certainly the case for me. I know from experience that if a marriage is having problems, differences of opinion in religion will exacerbate the troubles. I married very young, while my understanding about religion and God was still shifting considerably. My metamorphosis took me from a loosely attached Catholic to an agnostic. I had an awakening or an evolution of sorts, but my spouse at the time remained very loyal to his Baptist roots. When I started to speak up about my views, it caused a great deal of conflict.

If you're a believer, and you strongly believe that being anything but Christian will send you straight to hell, the mere presence of someone

---

[4] Riley, "Interfaith Unions," *New York Times* (April 5, 2013): A17.

who does not believe in God feels threatening. The more I dug in my heels about my views, the greater the rift became. I was told a few times—in an informative way, of course—that I was going to hell for my beliefs (or, rather, lack of them). Living with someone of such strong faith is wearing and difficult if you have none, and I'm sure it is difficult for the devout to live with partners who don't believe.

Religion, or lack of it, is not a trivial consideration, like hair or eye color. It's not a superficial trait; rather, it's a core set of beliefs, buried deep within our subconscious and conscious minds, that guides our words and our actions. On a daily basis, God is invoked—at meals, before bed, on Sundays, in times of crisis, and in judgment of others who don't believe. A secret dialogue ran continuously through my head with words like *silly* and *illogical*, thoughts that I could not and would not express out loud; I'm sure my spouse had his own words for me, too.

In all fairness, from the believer's point of view, she is taught from a young age that her way is the only way, and after years of reinforcement, it's hard for her to change. Souls are either saved or in the Devil's possession. For many of our nation's religions, there is no in between. If you believe in this stuff, really believe (and it's hard for you and me to put ourselves in these shoes), imagine how uncomfortable it must feel to know your loved one has been caught by the dark side. Your enemy literally sleeps in bed with you, and you'll be taking separate eternal vacations after you die. Moreover, one of the ways in which Christians can be redeemed is by converting and saving others. It becomes a personal mission (read: a nonstop ticket to heaven) to convert nonbelievers. I talked with some nonbelievers who said their spouses don't even know their true feelings about religion. To avoid conflict or harsh feelings—even divorce—some nonbelievers don't "come out," even to their partners.

Of course, interfaith marriages aren't always unhappy and don't always result in divorce. Most happy couples of mixed belief just live and let live: They accept their partners for how they are and don't feel the need to be "right" about religion. If your marriage survives intact after the first few years of wedded bliss and children are on the horizon, I would recommend sitting down beforehand and discussing how you'll raise the kids. Write it down. What will you tell (or not tell) them? Will you take your children to church as a family? How often? Will your children participate in the rites of your religion? Will you talk openly with them about opposing beliefs?

If you do find yourself in my position, and I know that a lot of people change their views about God later in life, raising kids with parents who stand so opposite in their views isn't necessarily a bad thing. If the parents remain respectful, especially in front of the kids, then the children have the opportunity to learn about religion firsthand while also having input from you. I've asked my kids a lot of questions over the years about the church services they attend. I just listen and withhold judgment—my goal is not to undermine their father but just to get them thinking, questioning. What was the sermon about? What are their thoughts? Do they believe that laying on of hands really helps cure kids of behavioral problems? Attending church services helps kids see the "other side," and gives them an understanding of how religion works.

ALICE'S STORY: RAISING DAUGHTERS IN HER HUSBAND'S FAITH

Alice grew up in an agnostic family. She lives in Texas and is married to someone who is a devout Christian. She shares her thoughts on marriage and on raising her daughters in her husband's faith:

My husband is Church of Christ. It's been a big thing in his family for years. I actually met him at church when I was visiting with a friend, ironically.

I have recently spoken to my eldest daughter (almost thirteen) about my doubts about God. Basically, I believe that if there is a God (I think that's unlikely) and he is good, then he's not going to throw a good person like me in some hell or whatever. A reverse Pascal's wager, if you will. I did worry that she'd be afraid for me, but I think she's okay. I've talked with her more about my disapproval of the role of women in that church (as in the submissive crap). I have a feeling she may not stick with that brand of Christianity if it doesn't get with the times fast. She's too much a feminist, like me.

She does like me to be there, so now I try to go on Sunday evenings sometimes. It is more laid-back then. (Oh, and they have church three times a week: Wednesday and twice on Sunday.) I ask them a lot of questions. We read about other religions (they especially love the Greek gods in a series called "Percy Jackson and the Olympians"). Basically, I want my children to be able to decide what they believe for themselves. They are both extremely smart and curious, so I think they'll do okay. If they can get the good things out of faith—the comfort and goodwill—then I will be very happy for them. I will be happy for them if they turn away as well. My biggest point with them is never to use religion to put someone down. I suffered that a lot as a kid. The whole "You're going to hell" bit.

Originally, I tried to convert to Christianity. My parents are mostly agnostic, and they dislike organized religion in general. We never went to church. But we live in the Bible Belt, so I tried to conform. There are actually very nice people in church. There are also some really awful ones. Yet around here, it's almost impossible to find a community organization that isn't somehow involved with a church. It's been very good for the girls because they've been able to make a lot of friends. So you learn to ignore all the "God" stuff as much as possible.

167

My husband is not a great thinker. This is not to say he's not intelligent; he just goes with the flow. He's a mechanic who works with his hands, not the philosopher like his wife, the English major. He is usually very supportive of me. He likes it when I go to church, but he doesn't guilt-trip me about not going. There have been some issues in the past. At one church we attended, he tended to always believe church members were saints and couldn't possibly have meant that mean thing they said. That really annoyed me. That's his blind spot—religion is Church of Christ and Church of Christ is church and church is God. You could say I have my own faith—in liberal politics. I get very political. Again, he just doesn't. He votes differently than I do, too, but it's not a major concern. He doesn't think about it—it just is for him. I don't put down religion around him and he doesn't harp on it constantly around me. We balance each other. Live and let live, I guess.

It hasn't always been easy, but honestly we fight more about stuff like money than we do about religion. He's just not confrontational about it. I was not a Christian when we met, and he loved me anyway. I think our personalities (uptight constant thinker and relaxed "just go with it" kind of guy) mesh well together. The problem comes when one of us thinks we need to "convert" the other—whether to atheism or religion. If there is respect involved, it can work. It's not easy, but no marriage is, and you have to make concessions for each other. We've been married fourteen years, so I guess so far that's what's worked for us. I can't say it will forever, but for now it does.

Love

'm going to tell you right now. As a human being, the way that the Christian God loves is not a model for me—it's not the way I want to be loved, to show love, or to teach my children how to love.

You hear it from so many people: God's love for us is perfect. God loves us because he forgives our sins. We do not deserve his love. We are huge failures; complete disappointments; dirty, sinful things. Blah blah blah. Why are we such losers? Because one man and one woman, a long, long time ago, did something so outrageous, so unforgivable that it ruined everything for everyone for all time. (Of course, you know that I don't believe this, but this is what many of us were taught growing up.) The father who was supposed to know all, create all, and love all designed the curiosity gene as part of our genetic makeup, gave us free will (sort of), and then, when we made a choice, given the options from our programming, God held it against us. Forever.

Talk about holding a grudge. I can't imagine any person being less forgiving and less loving than the God (Christian and otherwise) humans have created and refined through the ages. How does this God show his love? Not just to you, Mr. or Ms. Believer. I'm asking, objectively, how does God show his love for your neighbor? No, not the neighbor who was diagnosed with cancer and lost his house. God didn't love that guy. The other neighbor—you know, the one with the big BMW who worked for that telecom company and cashed out all his stock options before the business went belly-up. God clearly loved that guy for letting him get away with fraud. Wait. What? God doesn't get involved in our human affairs? Then why pray? And what about all those people who claim to be "saved" every year? How are they saved if God doesn't lift a finger or get involved? Or perhaps this is how God shows his love, objectively, for everyone. He helps no one.

Fortunately, you and I don't have to worry about things like that. We only love people who live here on planet earth, and there's a reason for that. Love for others is not invisible. You can see it. If we think of love as the emotion that makes us feel warm, safe, excited, or happy, we are focusing on ourselves. That's the response many people have to their perceived love affair with God: He makes me feel [fill in the blank]. They are focusing on their personal reaction, on how another person makes them feel. Don't get me wrong—these feelings are not bad. They are often automatic and subconscious responses, necessary to keep humankind working and thriving. But these feelings should not be the definition of love; they should be the by-products. Love is the way we talk to and treat one another. It is as observable as the people we love.

Unlike God, I'm not going to abandon those I love in their time of need. I'm not going to ignore my friends when they are heartbroken. I will listen and respond and put my hand on top of theirs. I will take my mother's phone call, no matter how busy I am, so that she knows I'm always here for her. I will help my elderly neighbor when I see her lying motionless on the sidewalk, rather than driving past her in a rush to play golf or tennis (true story). I will put $10 in my kid's backpack, knowing that he sometimes forgets his lunch, not on purpose, but because he's got a lot on his plate and on his mind.

We are animals; obviously, very complex animals. Emotions are the offspring, over thousands of years, of many aspects of human development: of bigger brains, of genes and chemicals that promote bonding between humans, of having moved past the stage in our development where all we thought about was eating, sleeping, and rutting. We have within each of us every human emotion possible, to a greater or lesser degree, but we prune and develop our emotional responses as we grow. We make choices. We choose to become who we are, and our response to others is one of the few things we have control over. It is also the way we show our humanity.

In teaching our children how to love others, we also teach them how to recognize love for themselves, perhaps one of the most important things we will teach them, not just for their well-being but also for a healthy, happy society. If we've brought our children up to understand what love is, to choose the actions and words that express love, then it becomes clear to them, when they start dating, that a guy or girl who calls them names or who berates them is *not* loving. I learned this the hard way after dating someone who said he "loved me to death." He was literally killing me with jealousy and rage and hurtful words. I had to learn that love is not some ideal "out there" or in our hearts. It's not chemistry or magic or men on white horses. It's in our behavior and our words.

Unlike God, we don't have to love everyone—we shouldn't love everyone. Love takes time and energy. If a person is unhealthy or hurtful or not a good fit, no matter what connection that person has with us, we can be cordial but not grow or sustain the relationship.

Social Networking Etiquette
for Nonbelievers

For years, I didn't use my real name when blogging for two main reasons. First, there are big nuts in the nut jar, and I didn't want to endanger my kids. Second, I knew that, should I be outed, some of the people I know would take offense. See, it's okay to preach to people—your friends, family, or strangers—about *your* belief in God and about other people's destiny if they *don't* believe, but it's not okay to tell people, "Sorry, I don't believe in God."

Believers, for the most part, take much greater offense to statements of disbelief than nonbelievers take to preaching. If you are a believer, you are free to say what you want because you are only trying to save others (yet, ultimately, yourself). You are doing a "good" thing, according to your preacher, your fellow Christians, and your God. (We know better). Never mind that someone might have his very own opinions. Everyone is supposed to copy each other, we learn in school: Copy this knowledge, remember so-and-so's findings, memorize what that person said. What they forgot to teach is this: Learn what makes sense, examine the sources, look at the context—not all of our knowledge base is correct, and it's constantly changing; what is poured in can be poured out. We're so used to having sh*t piled on us since birth that it's hard just to say, "Please stop the madness." Some people are already so crazy that they really do get mad at any challenges to their belief systems.

Fortunately, with Facebook, Twitter, and other social media, we do not *have* to participate in posts and tweets from others. So, for the physical and emotional safety of nonbelievers, as well as peace of mind, I recommend staying on the fringe and merely watching the show on social media. Poking a hornet's nest will just result in a bunch of angry insects. Unfortunately, the rhetoric doesn't die off after one sting; it simply grows more frenzied. We don't want to subject ourselves, and especially our children, to such nonsense.

One reason people cannot give God up is because they are afraid of being alone, afraid of the Grim Reaper. Or maybe they just can't live with uncertainty. Forgive them. Remember that all the stupid, mindless stuff people post online about God isn't about God anyway. It isn't about you or me. It's about them.

What sorts of comments are we talking about? Comments like these:

The word! It's as real today as yesterday and forever. He is coming back again. Please be ready, my friends.

And: *Wowwwww. . . . Woke up this morning with my mind on Jesus!!! Nothing else matters.*

And: *I was thinking last night to myself. . . . Maybe the reason the tragedy happened last week at Newtown is that God wants us to put HIM/Prayers back in the school instead of the policemen with guns. . . . Seems to me they're fighting fire with fire. . . . What is it going to take for people to believe we serve a True and Living God?*

While you might be thinking this: *Doesn't your loving God have a better way of telling people that he wants to get back in the schools? Who wants to love a God that sends that kind of message?*

You should say this: *[Nothing.]*

Misconceptions and Learning
to Live without Knowing

Not too long ago, I had a few friends over for dinner. One of the guests, a very Baptist woman, had no idea that I was nontheist. We had been friends for three years. Obviously, not close friends, but friendly enough that I knew where she worked, the details of her last breakup with a younger boyfriend, and the name of the church she attended on Wednesday nights and Sunday mornings. This sometimes happens to me: I'll know people for a while, will know their life stories, the churches they belong to, and one day they'll suddenly wonder what church I belong to. This has been a friendship breaker in the past, and, as I discuss in a later essay, that's okay.

So the conversation at dinner turned to church. Not sure how we got there, but I think it started when we didn't say grace before eating. I just didn't think about it, although my other guests, two Hindus and a nondenominational Christian, may have wanted a few words of thanks before eating.

"Aren't you all going to say a blessing?" my Baptist friend asked me.

We don't usually say grace, I said, *but we can now if you'll lead us.* My friend looked askance at me.

"What church do you belong to?" she asked. *I don't go to church,* I said. *I'm agnostic.*

"What?" she said. "Isn't that some kind of cult or something?"

No, I told her. *No cult. It just means that I don't believe in God or religion.* Hard-core believers sometimes find the idea of not believing difficult to wrap their mind around. Religion is faith. Agnosticism is a judgment of that faith. Religion is miracle and myth and hope for the future. Agnosticism is focused on the here and now and the sensible. It's learning to be comfortable with the uncomfortable.

"So you don't believe in God?" she asked as if she'd just tasted something bad, and it's quite possible that it was my cooking as much as my religious views. "Girl, you all need to come to my church. The preacher is totally different. He will win you over."

Of course, for those of us who don't believe, we know there is no "winning over." We don't want to be won over and we don't want to go back. *That's okay,* I said. *I'm all right. I used to be Catholic.*

The thing is, people will ask you questions, but a lot of times they already have their own answers. Or they ask but they don't really want to know; they only want an opportunity to talk more about their views.

I suddenly felt as if I had become a lottery ticket to heaven. If she could convince me to join her at church, she'd win the heavenly jackpot. I could tell that my departure from the religious norm was at once exciting and frightening to her. She was surely thinking, "What does a person believe in if not God? How can we be moral if we have no higher judge? How do you explain how we got here, this seemingly perfect world, why we have awareness?" The list is endless.

"But what about the *kids*? They need church. Don't you want them to go to heaven?" my friend asked.

The kids have been to different churches, I told her, *and they're okay with not going. Trust me. If I thought there were a heaven, I'd be the first in line with my kids.*

I knew that, no matter what I said, she wouldn't really understand. She can't. If she did, she wouldn't be a believer. If she could relate to what I was saying, she'd know that I just can't force myself—or my kids—to believe in something that doesn't make sense, that offers no proof or credibility. Some say they have proof, but they present evidence, like the Bible, that is not accepted as divinely inspired by those of us who don't believe. If there is or was a God, we have no way of knowing. Better people than me have tried.

My friend didn't know how many nights I stayed up worrying that I'd be harming my kids by bringing them up outside the norms of mainstream America. There were other issues, too, like acceptance. Kids without God? Some people would assume they'd be amoral. Would they have trouble in school or at work? One day, they'd find girlfriends—would they reject my kids because they have no belief?

"Well, why take a chance?" my friend asked. "It doesn't hurt to have faith." And I knew she meant well and believed what she said.

I've heard that argument before—Pascal's wager: It's better to hedge your bets and accept God. Of course, I'd be pretending to believe in a God who supposedly already knows my true thoughts, so it kind of defeats the purpose. What would I have to lose by worshipping God, even with doubts? That would make me one big fake, and that goes against everything I had taught my kids about being as real and as truthful as possible. My hedge was being agnostic—I don't believe in the God humans have created, yet I cannot, with certainty, claim to know if there is not or never was a God-force at some point, at some place. I can only say that I see no evidence of a supreme being now nor do I see evidence that the Bible provides us with any understanding of our origins or the origins of the universe. No, if I were to look at the Bible as anything more than a collection of flawed historical texts, I would only find a mean-spirited, illogical, and controlling God.

I tell my friend: *It's hard at first, but, as a nonbeliever, you learn to live without explanations, without reasons, without the safety net of a promised afterlife. You learn to be okay with being uncomfortable.*

That's the crux of living without belief, of teaching our kids to live without God. We learn to be okay and we learn that we *will* be okay—as okay as any other person, Christian or not, who lives alongside us. No lightning bolt will strike us dead for not believing. No Devil will inhabit our bodies and make us his zombie soldiers. Possessions and exorcisms are magical leftovers of the medieval church. The Devil doesn't even make the list of those to fear—it's the people who fill the church I'm afraid of.

My friend shakes her head and doesn't say anything else. She's been caught off guard, coming to my house, not knowing that we are heathens. It can be frustrating: I knew her faith, and she was welcome at my table. I know she's wondering how quickly she can bolt out the door after eating. It's the last time we'll share a meal together.

RITUALS
▪ AND ▪
HOLIDAYS

Mystery and
Creating Rituals

When I was a kid, I was enamored of the Catholic Church. My mother used to walk my brother and me across the street and up the long grassy hill to our church. She was raised a strict Catholic. An Italian Catholic. She made sure that we never missed a Sunday or a holy day. She taught—and took us to—CCD for religious education, and through the usual sacramental rites for neophytes.

There was always mystery inside the church. The red glow of prayer candles as you walked in, the holy water by the door, the distinctive smells of Catholicism—incense and oils and an aging building. The wooden pews and the stained-glass windows. The Stations of the Cross and the images of a tortured Jew. The secret tabernacle where the host was stored. The confessionals. So much secrecy and silence. You had to whisper in church, even when it was empty, as if someone or something were sleeping.

To this day, if I don't think too hard, I can still recite the prayers of the mass, even though my mind often wandered as a child. Through rote memorization, I learned every word the priest would say. I was indoctrinated slowly, every Sunday of my first fifteen or so years of life. That's why the churches bring the children in as babes, before they are even aware of what is happening or what the words mean, before they know to question authority.

As a child, I felt a sense of peace and calmness as I sat there with my mother, bored, watching the colored light come through the stained glass. Had the nuns provided pillows, I would surely have fallen asleep. I had been cleansed and forgiven and had eaten the body and blood of Christ, and I was safe beside my mother in her place of worship. God is good, God is great was our mantra. Brainwashing is subtle and sounds a lot like a lullaby. We sang songs that would stick in my head for days.

My children have missed this mystery and this comfort—and this brainwashing. At first, I did feel bad about the rituals, the rites of passage, they would never experience. I believed for a while that I took this from my children. But what I thought I was taking was not real—it was only a false sense of safety created by myths and by doing the same thing over and over and over again in a place that was deemed sacred by the adults in my life. There was no one, no God or priest or nun, who would provide for my children's safety, no one who would love them no matter what they said or did—except me. My children would be no safer in a church than at home.

Mystery, sometimes, is nothing more than secrecy. In the Catholic Church, with its decades of scandals, that is certainly true. Mystery doesn't have to be artificially induced by religion. We can teach our kids to enjoy the true wonders and mysteries around them: the language of ants, the formation of clouds, the amazing engineering of our ears. We don't have to trick or brainwash our kids into thinking that God and the church keep us safe or hold the answers. We don't *have* to have all the answers. The reality is that no one knows what exists, if anything, before life is created and after a body dies—not even priests and preachers. Not knowing is not only OK, but also a way to remain open to all possibilities and views. My son used to ask me all the time, "Mom, if the universe is expanding, what is it expanding into?" I do not know, but we came up with some interesting possibilities.

We can create our own rituals, too, in our homes. A Sunday morning habit of sitting down together and having discussions over a cup of hot chocolate creates many opportunities to learn and help children grow. Making pancakes together, seeing a matinee, biking, crafts, or playing board games on Sundays make memories that kids will remember for years. Anything deemed special to the family and repeated over and over becomes a tradition. What really gives kids a sense of security is knowing that every member of their family is important, every opinion is valued, and that, inside the safety of their home, love is given but not taken away. It's knowing that we will be loved, no matter how many times we fall from grace.

Church Manners
and Old Rules

One mom from Pennsylvania wrote, "I have no problem with my children attending services for other religions. My experience has been that kids raised in freethinking families tend to find the services either boring and pointless or interesting from an educational perspective but not something they want to do often."

It's going to happen. Over a holiday or after a sleepover at a friend's house, you or your children will be asked to come to church. I think it's beneficial to attend mass with family or friends for several reasons. First, I like to show my support because, even though I'm not a believer, I do believe in the right to worship. In fact, I'd rather go to a church than have a friend bring her church to me, if you know what I mean. Attending church helps broaden my kids' experiences, inform them about religious views, and encourage tolerance. Second, it's always interesting to see what the big deal is, why people want to be part of their chosen religion. Third, sometimes the clergyperson actually gives a really good sermon that is germane to everyday life. Fourth, church interiors are aesthetically pleasing: the symbols or the lack of, the stained glass, the flowers, the smells and the artwork. And, finally, I sometimes just enjoy a few moments to sit and listen to soothing music and hushed tones. Of course, not all churches are like this—some church services are held in school cafeterias and some have Christian rock bands that jar you awake on Sunday mornings. But you get the idea—attending church can be enlightening for us, and it is important to our friends and families. It's a kind gesture to attend *on occasion*, if you're asked.

Going to church is an experience, just like attending a wedding or visiting the zoo. We get to witness humans comforting themselves and each other. And out of respect, we rise, sit, kneel, and line up on cue. When it comes time to say the Lord's Prayer, we silently bow our heads and listen to the drone of sleepy and bored voices. We wait in the pews while our family and friends walk to the front of the church to take their swig of wine or juice and politely chew their little white wafers.

While I'm talking about wafers, also called the Host, sacramental bread, or Communion bread, depending on which branch of Christianity you're part of, I thought I'd throw in a few interesting historical tidbits. In Catholicism, where the bread and wine mania started, the belief is that transubstantiation occurs during mass. Catholic doctrine states, whether Catholics realize or even believe it, that the Host truly becomes the body of Christ when the priest says his magical words during mass. It's a miracle over and over again. Jesus is trapped in a version of the movie *Groundhog Day*. The wine—really good red wine, I might add—actually becomes Christ's blood. Through some mystical process, although there is no change in outward appearance, the altar bread and wine indeed become Christ the sacrificial victim. Gross thought, right? How do church officials even rationalize this? They don't. I think some followers just don't know all the Catholic dogma, having been taken in as babies, or they simply reject the parts they don't agree with. How can foodstuffs be transformed into a being while still looking like bread? I can't say I blame Catholics for rejecting some of these irrationalities while still wanting to feel warm, fuzzy, and hopeful. If you were brought up in the church and have a fondness for it, why throw the baby out with the holy water?

You can see, however, especially in Christianity, that religion has transitioned from its place of magic and supernatural powers. We are still a superstitious people, but our churches are not the same awe-inspiring places of worship with outrageous practices (megachurches not included). They've evolved, just as we have. We no longer believe, as was thought in medieval times, that the Host can be used to encourage bees to make honey, cure the blind, or protect criminals from discovery.[5] The sacramental wafer had to be placed by the priest directly on the communicant's tongue because, up through the sixteenth century, people had been known to sneak the Host from the church to use in cures, miracles, charms, and even for harmful purposes.[6]

When the Protestant Reformation came along, it brought a much less magical, stripped-down, more (relatively) rational concept of religion. Shortly thereafter, science came to the fore, first to prove that God existed and then to disprove the existence of God. Rituals, such as baptism, first communion, and confirmation, are now important as celebratory rites of passage, rather than as signs of God's grace.

Of course, unlike Martin Luther, these are the things I keep to myself before, during, and after church. What kind of church manners would I have if I said that Communion is a holdover from the age of magic? I taught my children that it's okay to question and make comments about

---

[5] Keith Thomas, *Religion and the Decline of Magic* (Oxford, UK: Oxford University Press, 1997), pp. 34–35.

[6] Thomas, p. 35.

their church experiences, but only to me—because I won't be offended. We had to learn this the hard way when my eighty-something-year-old grandmother took offense at one of her grandson's remarks after mass. There's a rule that's older than God: Never offend any person who has "grand" or "great-grand" in front of her title.

Happy Meal Baptism

Though we had baptized the children as infants into Catholicism, after we split, my children's father wanted to bring the kids into his new fold. (*Fold* [as noted in *Merriam-Webster*]: *An enclosure for sheep.*) And, naturally, his new house of worship was none other than our town's biggest Baptist church, the church with its own fitness facility and indoor basketball courts, the church that has more amenities than any of our local hotels. Let me just say that, regardless of our differences in religion, I realize that he was only doing what he believed was best, and I appreciate the love and devotion he has for our kids.

My older kid did not want to be baptized again. He considered the church's pastor to be a leader and a businessman in his congregation. He noted that the preacher was the only person "interpreting" the Bible on his own, and, for this, my kid told me, the pastor "makes tons of money." Preachers are spiritual capitalists, and he was already wary of churches.

It was the younger child, at eight years old, whose soul was being pawned. As much as I didn't mind his going to church, the idea that he would be inducted via dunking in front of all those Stepford Baptists sort of bugged me. Who would do the reaping? The church, of course. They were adding another sheep, expecting that he would one day grow up to share financial responsibility for the preacher and his house of God.

So I asked my son, *Why are you being baptized?* And, as a younger sibling will often do, he replied to me, "I don't know. Ask my brother."

Do you know what it means to be baptized? I asked.

"No," he told me. "I learned one time, but I forgot."

The Catholics catch hell for baptizing babies who are so young their heads wobble around like Regan, the possessed girl from *The Exorcist*, whose mother was, of course, one of those unsavory atheists. But you and I know the real reason infants are baptized is so that no other religion can get to them first. Babies are new customers, which means another lifetime of revenue or even, if the church is lucky, a priest or nun. In my opinion, baptizing an eight-year-old who does not fully understand what baptism means is worse than baptizing a helpless infant who has no clue what is going on. At least the infant won't remember getting up in front of a large group of strangers with plastic smiles because he had to be saved from his dirty, sinful self.

The big baptism happened anyway; I went to pick up my children from their dad's house after the deed was done. It was my birthday and we were going to eat at Jinbeh, a Japanese restaurant my younger son loved. He was very excited when I arrived, but not because we were going to see an elaborate show with fire and knives. He was excited because one of the members of his dad's church had stopped by with a gift for his baptism.

If a church can't guilt a child into membership, if the elders can't pull him in with fear or with approval of his sinning self or promises of life ever after, they'll draw him in with doughnuts and gifts.

What would be an appropriate gift for the baptism of a child who was one month shy of nine years old? I would think a cross, a pocket Bible, or some other symbolic trinket. No, what my kid received was a large toy car: a metal, deep-blue, snazzy replica of a Dodge Viper. I thought of golden arches and snappy jingles, hamburger meals that come complete with a bonus toy. What does a Dodge Viper have to do with baptism into the holy world of Jesus Christ?

There was a clue in my older son's behavior. He was excited, too. He demonstrated all the moving parts: the trunk opened to expose a spare, removable tire. He lifted the hood to reveal a shiny silver engine. Then he stood up and smiled. "Maybe I'll get baptized, too."

Like toys packaged with fast food hamburgers, baptismal toys entice kids to eat a lot of crap.

They Had Good Food

When your religious beliefs start to unravel, the fabric of what you believe is never quite the same, no matter how hard you try to put it back together. It's like a four-inch tear in your favorite cotton shirt. It will just never look the same again once it's stitched up. This was true for me. It seemed to be true for my younger kid.

Introducing critical thinking and common sense consistently and often into a child's life will eventually cause him to shun religion for himself (though, hopefully, not as a topic of study). I've seen a progression in my son's religious beliefs from blindly accepting religion to forming his own ideas. A little over a year after he was baptized for a second time, it started with this statement, which I wrote down verbatim in my calendar:

"I'm going to tell Dad that I wasn't ready to be baptized. I don't know why I did that. They had good food, I guess. I believe in God, but not heaven or hell."

These remarks followed on the heels of a discussion about hell. *Where it could be? Up? Down? What does it look like? How did it get there? How do you get there from here?* (Elevator, down. Please.) *Does it even make sense,* I asked my son. He thought about these things briefly before coming to the conclusion that, No, none of it really made sense.

He added, "It also doesn't make sense that God can hear everyone's prayers. It would be like a busy restaurant. You can't hear everyone talking at the same time." Not a bad analogy, I thought. It's hard enough for me to hear both my kids talking to me at once. "And what about airplanes, right?"

What about them? I said.

"When airplanes fly into the sky, it would be so noisy in heaven." Then he reminded me that telescopes had not seen any heaven, nor had rocket ships. All true, I told him.

If given the chance, children will tear away the wrapping of their religious beliefs as if it were a birthday present. It takes time, but it will happen.

He "Decides"

I wrote an earlier essay about allowing my sons to choose their own religion. They've been to Catholic and Baptist churches; we've read and talked about the Bible and about all the major religions, past and present. I told them my views, and we've discussed arguments from philosophers who don't believe in God. For critics who worry that I've tainted my kids—made them bait for the Devil—I'm sure I have, but they've also been tainted—or saved—by their friends and family members who believe, too. So I guess it all evens out in the end because they are equally influenced by believers and nonbelievers. At some point, I figure they will have the emotional maturity and the information they need to decide for themselves what they do or do not believe.

One night, after sitting down to dinner on the patio outside, my newly eleven-year-old son said, "I'm diagnostic."

My older kid started laughing.

You know what he means, I said, trying to kick him under the table.

I asked, *Why did you decide to be agnostic?*

"Because I just don't know," the eleven-year-old told me. "I just can't be sure. Everyone believes different things."

Well, that's a start. I figure as long as he's thinking, that's a good thing. Do I think he really is "diagnostic"? Of course not. It'll be years before he figures out if he is or is not. As he shuffles more relationships and more information into his life, hopefully he'll be diagnosing what he believes, over and over again.

Giving Thanks

I n a country that has no wars on its soil, that has plenty of food, electricity, and opportunities for education, we have so much. We should be giving thanks every day. How do we teach our kids to be thankful when we're raising them without God? It's not hard to do. Being grateful means that we express our appreciation for some kindness or benefit that has been given to us. We don't *have* to know its source—only that we realize we are fortunate, and we are humble enough to know that it's not our doing.

When believers sit down to dinner and thank God, some do so with the fear that their good fortune will be taken from them if they don't show appreciation. If they don't give proper thanks, they may not get another hot meal; they may not go to heaven. Nonbelievers have the luxury of just being thankful.

This is what our family does—or used to do when we all had time to sit down for meals together. At dinner, we'd take turns saying what we're thankful for: the sun, the rain, the kindness of strangers, our good health, siblings, dogs, tennis balls—the list is very long. I'd tell my kids that I have no idea how we got here, but I'm so grateful for this life experience we're sharing, for the food we have, and for a warm bed at night. Then I'd ask them what they appreciate about each other. Usually, it was just, "He plays with me." Sometimes they were silly, and sometimes they would just say, "I don't know." And that's okay because at least they are thinking about gratitude for others.

One atheist mother I met says her family gives thanks like this:

> *Each night at dinner we say one thing we are thankful for that day in our efforts to try to build an attitude of gratitude and to remind us that our lives are good. For more formal family gatherings, we sing the first stanza of an old blessing song called Johnny Appleseed. Wherever the words "the Lord" are used, we substitute "the world." So instead of singing, "Oh, the Lord is good to me," we say, "the world is good to me." I believe being thankful to the world is much more meaningful than thanking some deity that no one can prove exists.*

I learned the "Johnny Appleseed" song in Girl Scouts. If you can't remember the tune, I'm sure you can find some kid singing her version on YouTube. Here's the nonbeliever's version (all stanzas):

> *Oh, the world's been good to me.*
> *And so I thank the world*
> *For giving me the things I need:*
> *The sun, the rain and the appleseed;*
> *Oh, the world's been good to me.*
>
> *Oh, and every seed I sow*
> *Will grow into a tree.*
> *And someday there'll be apples there*
> *For everyone in the world to share.*
> *Oh, the world is good to me.*

Oh, here I am 'neath the blue, blue sky
Doing as I please.
Singing with my feathered friends
Humming with the bees.

I wake up every day,
As happy as can be,
Because I know that with its care
My apple trees, they will still be there.
The world's been good to me.

I wake up every day
As happy as can be,
Because I know the world is there
Watchin' over all my friends and me
The world is good to me.

Agnostic Prayers

This is what an agnostic's prayer should not sound like:

O Lord, Oh, you are so big, so absolutely huge. Gosh, we are all just absolutely impressed down here, I can tell you. Forgive us, Lord, for our dreadful toadying and barefaced flattery. But you are so strong and, well, just so super. Fantastic. Amen.

—The chaplain's prayer from
Monty Python's *The Meaning of Life*

Most of us find ourselves having to give or receive a blessing before a meal. At the end of every school year, my son's tennis team has a banquet. Three out of the last four years, a Christian prayer has been offered up before eating. This year the coach, aware that we had two Muslim players on the team, wanted to find a blessing that would not offend anyone. So I volunteered to write a few words of gratitude that were inclusive to both believers and nonbelievers. You can change it any way you like for your specific needs:

Let us be thankful for this food, for the time to celebrate together, and for the special memories we've created with the team this year.

If you have the chance to offer up a neutral "prayer" for your group or family, there are many ways to get around mentioning God or Jesus. Just write a few lines about what or whom you appreciate. To whom should you be thankful? Listeners can decide for themselves. God. Allah. Nature. Mom and Dad. The chef. What are you thankful for? Time together, good health, plenty of food, peace in the family, a new baby? You can tailor your thankfulness to a specific audience.

For example, this "prayer" would be good for a more intimate gathering, such as Thanksgiving:

Let's take a moment to touch hands and reaffirm our connection to each other. We will enjoy this meal together in friendship. Thank you to the host [or hostess] for the time and energy you took to bring this food to the table, and thank you to our guests for taking the time to join us and share a meal.

As nonbelievers, we just want to make sure that we don't insult others' beliefs by being antagonistic or derogatory. And if someone does add a "praise the Lord" or a "thank you, sweet Jesus," it won't be any more painful than a sprinkling of fairy dust. The best we can do is offer up our tolerance through a respectful silence.

You might be thinking, "Well, they're not being very respectful of us." Perhaps, but it's more likely that they just are so convinced their way is the right way and only way. If you are inside a locked box, you won't be able to see what's outside. I look at praying like this: If a person thinks Coke is better than Pepsi, good for him. I have no desire to engage in argument. In fact, I don't even drink soda. When a person pushes me to drink his soda, I firmly tell him no thanks, but if someone just wants to take a few moments to tell me how great his soda is, then that should be okay. Now just substitute God or Allah for soda.

That Silly Santa—
I Mean, Satan

You wonder why people don't take responsibility for their own actions. Perhaps it has something to do with perpetuating the idea that "The Devil made me do it." How do we know if someone works for the evil one? Are these folks on the Devil's payroll? If so, I wonder what kinds of benefits they get.

As a parent, I try to steer my kids clear of people who believe that the Devil is real. Unfortunately, these men and women have children, and those children go to school with my kids. In elementary school, my sons used to come home afraid, scared by some of the kids at school and their stories of the Devil. You know the stereotypes often portrayed in movies—the Devil lives in the ground and he can reach up and grab your legs. Any little bump or stump in the dirt is a Devil finger poking through, just waiting for you to walk by.

Several times I explained to my kids that these are just Christian fear tactics. This is the way religion keeps its members: uniting the "good" against the "bad" or the unknown. Everyone loves the idea of an enemy.

I used to be worried that my kids would be scared into believing, but then I realized that children are actually very logical. I talked to them about the "Devil." Does the story make sense? How would the Devil breathe, and what does he look like? Does he live in one spot or travel underground? Should we dig up some dirt and see what is under there?

I asked them: If the Christian God, which your friends speak of, is so good and so powerful, why would he create an evil force that he cannot control? Have you ever seen the Devil? (I mean, seriously.) Do you really think a red man with horns is going to poke his hand out of the ground and drag you under? (A kid really said this.)

It takes years of brainwashing to turn kids into preaching, fearful adults. But if you get to them while they're young, they can still be saved.

Celebrating Christmas

Christmas isn't just for Christians. But I didn't need to tell you this. We all know that the exact date—and even the year—of Jesus Christ's birth is not known. Early Christians didn't even celebrate his birth until the ninth century. We also know that early Christianity usurped this date from pagan religions in hopes of gaining converts.

Do I celebrate Christmas? Hell, yes. The days are colder and darker. The nights arrive earlier and last longer. I have no problem punctuating our long hibernation with a bit of celebration. Dreary, gray yards get a cheery boost from Christmas lights and animated reindeer decorations. There are great memories to be made: Rudolph and Frosty, gingerbread houses, Christmas tree decorating, seasonal music, hot chocolate and sugar cookies, and books like *The Polar Express*. Who says religious belief is a requirement to participate in the festivities?

What greater fun is there than watching your kids decorate the tree or wrap presents? In my family, Christmas and birthdays are the only two times during the year that we could ask for gifts—and then, for Christmas, we can only ask for one from Mom and one from Santa. While our neighbors across the street stockpile a long laundry list of gifts for each kid, mine have a meager two (and a stocking, of course). That is my attempt at reining in the materialistic drunkenness that occurs in many American households on Christmas day and the ensuing disenchantment with all those toys that were supposed to bring happiness, but actually create indifference and a lack of appreciation. I don't think my kids ever felt they missed out on anything, and still, as teenagers, they only ask me for one gift.

So, yes, we celebrate Christmas, and when my kids were very young, I told them about Santa just as I told them about Mickey Mouse and Cinderella and all the other wonderful characters we encounter on our journey through childhood. And when my older son flat-out asked me if Santa was real, I told him that legend says there was once a very kind man named St. Nicholas who gave gifts to children and, after he died, parents wanted to continue the tradition. But, no, there aren't any flying reindeer or elves in the North Pole making toys. Santa—like the Easter Bunny—is a fun idea and a mythical character, rather than a real person. When my son learned about the myth behind the Santa story, he also learned the responsibility of keeping the truth to himself. It was not his place to tell other kids what he knew—it was a parent's job.

Christmas is a good time for a lesson on giving, though we should be teaching those lessons every day. As nonbelievers, we're not organized into communities—many of us are isolated and scattered around the fringe of society, but there are plenty of ways to reach out around us and spread cheer or help out in some way, whether it's through donating our time or donating our money. Each year, at my kids' schools, we'd pick a family from the angel tree, and we'd shop together for presents. Through this process, my kids learned that you buy for others not what *you* want but what you think they want. A gift is not much of a gift if the recipient doesn't want it. Then there were the Christmas cookies or zucchini bread we baked for our friends and neighbors because giving stuff, in a society that already has too much stuff, doesn't mean much.

One agnostic mom who used to be a Jehovah's Witness said that she and her children enjoy using the extra time once consumed by church during the holidays for volunteering. "It's something JWs do not do, since they consider their preaching work 'community volunteer service.' They are discouraged from volunteering and getting involved in any type of charitable good works. One of the first things I did upon leaving was join my student union and then volunteer on the board of a major mental health organization. My daughters volunteer for arts and music events, too. It's great to have not just the time to do these things, but the mental and emotional freedom."

The Reason
for the Season

It's no secret that Christmas in America suffers a bit from schizophrenia. Each year my neighbor's yard (like so many others in our city) has a neon sign that says, "Jesus is the reason for the season." Yet he also has in his yard a large figure of Santa with his reindeer. So the reason is what, I wonder? You'd think he'd be able to put two and two together: magical reindeer, a flying sleigh, and a man who's not real (Santa, that is). Both Santa and Jesus Christ have performed many a miracle, the largest being delivering presents to every child in one night, every year without fail. I'm a little confused as to why children get so many gifts on someone else's birthday anyway, and, if we want kids to think that Jesus is the reason for the season, why isn't Jesus the reason gifts appear under the tree? Shouldn't he be driving the sleigh?

It seems to me that entangling the commercialized holiday with the religious holy day just makes a mockery of the latter. Talk about confusing our kids: We teach them that Christmas is a sacred day for many in our country, but it is also a day of feral consumerism. The two seasons run parallel, culminating on December 25 (kind of).

And I really don't understand why church folks haul Jesus and the Wise Men from the local Walmart just to plop them in front of a school or a courthouse or a gas station. Is this a territorial thing or an advertisement? Wouldn't it be more significant, more sacred, if baby Jesus were only permitted on the property of authorized dealers, just as Apple only allows its sanctified products to be sold by approved businesses?

I'm not nearly the grump I seem. I know—my kids know—that we live in a Christian society. We have to be respectful of others' beliefs. Just as we don't want to be preached to, believers don't want to be told their God is a myth or is not real. In Texas, where we feel it's not only our right but our duty to put Jesus Christ back in Christmas, if an unsuspecting soul tells me, "Merry Christmas," I just smile and say, *Yeah, thanks. You, too.* In keeping with the season, a little indulgence for the religious doesn't hurt us.

When it comes to holidays with the family, the same sort of indulgence is necessary. The reason for the season, for nonbelievers, is to enjoy the camaraderie of family and friends. In order to do that, not only do we have to be tolerant, but we must often be part of religious traditions. This is not a bad thing, for it spreads goodwill and teaches our children how others celebrate.

■

MARIAN'S STORY: HOW SHE CELEBRATES CHRISTMAS

Marian grew up Mormon but is now raising her children as nonbelievers. At Christmas, she still participates in religious traditions and is careful to keep her views about religion to herself. She says it helps to ignore differences for the sake of family peace:

I still follow family traditions, some of which are Mormon, such as our own method of "family home evening" (not really a holiday, but a tradition that we carry on secularly); and we participate in secular celebrations of holidays. This includes making sure we are with extended family, and we always eat, and often will play games and sing together, and take time to sit as a family and enjoy chatting with each other. My mom continues to make the nativity scene with chocolate, as she always did when I was a child. But the meaning of it has changed. As my children have gotten older (I have a six-year-old son, a five-year-old daughter, and a nine-month-old daughter), they are asking questions about what religion we are. They aren't really exposed to Mormons here in Louisville—lots of Baptists, though! So I am telling my big kids the biblical stories (such as why people celebrate Easter and how), but I remind them that people can't really come back to life and we have no way of knowing if the stories are fiction or nonfiction. And I tell them they cannot talk about the stories with their friends, since, at this age, those stories are for grown-ups to tell their own children.

When we celebrate holidays with my half brother and half sister and their families (who are still Mormon), we all respect each others' religions, but I never ever speak to anyone in my family about being a nonbeliever. We spent Christmas together with all siblings and kids (sixteen people in all) a few years ago and I had a great time, and when it came time to pray before dinner and talk about the Mormon traditions of Christmas, I participated out of respect. So this particular holiday was wonderful, actually. It was the bringing together of people who barely knew each other and were of very different religious and political backgrounds, and the mutual respect and ignoring of our differences made the experience good, memorable. I guess one of the things I like about Mormons in my experience is they have no problem just letting me be who I am. Perhaps they go back to the church and send missionaries to my house (missionaries can find me wherever I live now!), but they are not confrontational. Religious confrontation scares me. I've learned from my mistakes, and learned that if people who are believers find out that I am not, they take it personally. So I only volunteer my atheism if someone else brings it up first.

Hearsay

Not long after my older child figured out that Santa Claus was a fake, he started questioning religion, tearing at the thin layer of belief in God and heaven that I had spread over him. It seemed like a natural progression. If there was no fat man who flew through the sky one night a year and delivered toys, was there a bearded old man sitting somewhere in the sky, smiling down on us, ready to smite us if we were naughty? If Kris Kringle didn't watch us all year long to make sure we were good (or bad), was there a God who sat in heaven and judged our actions?

Maybe some kids are just born to question how things work. My son was very interested in the universe and the planets. After he entered school, he began asking me where God might be and where heaven was. Then he asked me about things that didn't make sense to him (or me). How do we "know for sure" that Jesus was sent by God to save us? How do we know if Christ was even real? How do we know what God looks like if no one has ever seen him? (Don't worry, kid, he's an old, bearded, white guy who looks like your grandpa.) At that point, I just told him: I have no answers. I didn't even have any good ideas. To tell him definitively one way or another was wrong. I didn't know for certain if there was or was not a God. It doesn't seem likely to me. I didn't know for certain that Christ existed, and if he did, if he was divine: It's all hearsay. Most everything in life he will learn will be hearsay—information, stories, studies, details—passed from one person to another.

Milk and Cookies
for Santa

One December, I was reading one of those free, environmentally unfriendly magazines that arrive, unwanted, in the mail. This one was called *Living Magazine*. A lot of money went into producing its thick, glossy, full-color pages. I get one every month, and I think, What a huge waste of energy and resources. Then I toss it into the recycle bin. I've e-mailed folks in the magazine's circulation department and asked to be removed from their list not once, but three times.

I just happened to flip through one issue to see what type of information (and advertisements) was worth spending the money on. I stopped on the article called "Countdown to Christmas" to see why someone's Christmas to-do list could merit a two-page spread. I thought my atheist and agnostic friends would appreciate this: Under the subtitle "Things to Do Christmas Eve," the first important item to do in the five-item list is to bake a cake for Jesus. The fifth thing to do is this: "Don't forget milk and cookies for Santa."

Need I say more? Okay, I will. Does the same parent who eats the milk and cookies left for an imaginary man also get to eat the birthday cake left for an imaginary man? Why do parents stop believing in the former but not the latter?

Easter Candy

Why do you think that so many Christian families wake up to Easter baskets? How do these baskets full of cheap chocolate, sticky marshmallows and chewy jelly beans relate to Christ rising from the dead? Do we not see how susceptible we are to marketing, whether it's from businesses or churches? Target sells Easter candy. First Baptist sells God. What's the difference? One's a tangible product, the other intangible. One is full of calories; the other is full of hope. Just the same, we buy both.

I guess it seems odd that Christians, who believe that Easter is such an important day, will go out and buy baskets full of candy to celebrate Christ's rising from the dead. They will tell their children that the candy is from the "Easter Bunny," the invisible little furry animal that can, like Santa, haul ass all night to deliver confections. Then these same Christians will take their children to church where they will pray to God, the invisible old man who can hear every single prayer at once, who can reach down and into our lives on a whim if and when he feels like it.

For heathens like me, Easter always gave me an excuse to buy my kids a bag of dark chocolate, which is supposed to have antioxidants, and some books or a kite. I'd buy the gooey marshmallow bunnies for myself and hide them in the back of the pantry, where they usually petrified in their little carton homes because I'd forgotten about them.

Once Easter morning, after I told my kids Happy Easter Bunny Day, I asked them if it made sense that a big bunny breaks into everyone's house overnight to leave candy. They thought that was funny. Then I asked them if it made sense that a person can rise from the dead. They talked about dead animals. Dead bugs. Dead trees. None of these come back to life. *Yet trees do come back in the spring,* I said. My kids were quiet for a moment, and the younger one stood with his belly poking out because he was four years old and thought it was funny. And the other kid said, "*Maybe a person can come back to life if he really wasn't dead to begin with.*"

Easter without Religion

We run into the same issues with Easter as we do with Christmas. If you're a nonbeliever or an ex-believer, do you still celebrate Easter? I do.

When businesses give us an extra day off, they don't ask if we're believers in Christ. In all fairness, Christians rule when it comes to holidays. We should really be given a certain number of floating holidays per year, to be used for any celebration of our choosing, religious or not.

For now, we celebrate Easter because what we're really looking at is a secular holiday with the Easter Bunny *and* a religious holy day for Christ's rebirth. We all know that Easter was first a pagan holy day, usurped (again) by the Christians as a way to gain converts. Historians admit that they're not certain of the actual date of Christ's birth nor the exact date he rose from the dead. And I often wonder, if you're not sure when Jesus Christ was born or when he died, how can you be certain of what he said or if he was even one single person, named JC, or if he was two people, one named Jesus and one named Christ. But that's neither here nor there. The point is Christians are celebrating what they believe is an important event in their history. And many times, they, too, are celebrating the secular holiday as well with Easter egg hide-and-seek and tacky baskets filled with cheap candy.

Easter is a movable holiday—the first Sunday after the first full moon after the vernal equinox. Something I learned in college, but have since forgotten which class. Luckily, a moon fell into our planetary mix so that we can have high tides and surfing and songs about blue moons. Easter has always been a celebration of renewal. It seems like a more appropriate day for resolutions than New Year's, since this is a time when we, too, are renewed after emerging from a long, cold winter slumber. (Depending, that is, on where you live and how warm you keep your house.) Before we holed up in our houses and went from warm home to warm car to road to warm building and back, there was man and woman and maybe a baby in a papoose, walking the earth, looking to the sky, their bible, for indications of when to plant, when to expect the weather to warm.

Every spring, if we were plants or animals, we'd start to stretch and move around, the plants toward the sun and the animals in search of food and mates. Indeed, some of us are still in our spring while others are in our fall or winter. As much as we've separated ourselves from nature, we're animals, too, and our insides are still programmed to respond to the change in seasons, the comings and goings of night and day and monthly cycles.

For Christians and nonbelievers alike, Easter is not only a time to celebrate another spring, another season—no matter what our age—but for a rebirth of some sort. This is a time to renew the commitment to ourselves, our health, our children, our marriages, our friends, and even our gardens. It's also a time to buy our kids the candy that we never buy during the year.

It was always a joke at my house that one Easter, one of us would dress like Jesus, with the crown of thorns and wound marks, and wander into a church. Of course, these days, no one would believe we were sent from God. In Texas, we'd probably be shot. There could be no new Jesus now because we don't need one. In this country, we have met our basic needs for food, shelter, and medical care—we have reached (at least, most of us have) self-actualization. Two thousand years ago we needed JC to give us hope; now we need zombies to give us entertainment.

Yet on Easter, what I look forward to most is spending the day with family and friends, who will have us over for the usual Easter brunch after they attend mass in the morning. We will hide eggs for the little ones and pour wine for the big ones (that would be the adults). Any day that gives me extra time to relax and spend with the people I care about makes me happy, no matter if it's a holy day or everyone's holiday.

An Easter Story:
Forgiveness and Little Things

The family and I went out to eat one Easter around 1:00 p.m., which is prime time for the church folks, too. Where I live, the busiest time for restaurants isn't Friday or Saturday night: It's Sunday afternoon after the churches release their flocks.

You'd think, being Easter, people would be especially kind, particularly to their families. But every weekend, I see someone dressed up in their Sunday finery, reminding me that some folks can be groveling, self-centered creatures no matter what they call themselves.

But I digress. A young family sat beside us at lunch. The boy was around six and the girl, three or four perhaps. The boy was reaching for his napkin when he spilled his orange juice all over the table. His mother jumped up and became irate, telling him he was sloppy and careless. She cleaned the kid up while the boy frantically repeated his apology again and again and again. Both parents were unmoved by his sorrow. For at least ten minutes, they went on about the kid's irresponsibility, about how he doesn't pay attention. You'd think he'd just stolen money from the church poor box.

I wondered what it was like for this kid at home. The mother, with the scowl on her face, looked like she could be really nasty behind closed doors, and the dad looked as if he were wired really tightly. I thought about how many times, as an adult, I've spilled a drink. No one comes out yelling that I'm a bad person or that I'm sloppy or irresponsible, but that's what this kid was learning. Accidents made him a bad kid. Mom and Dad will get irrationally angry if he makes a mistake.

For Easter, that kid was learning how to parent with anger instead of kindness. For Easter, he was learning how not to forgive, not even for the littlest of things.

■

AMY'S STORY: HOW SHE CELEBRATES RELIGIOUS HOLIDAYS

Nonbelievers and their families come in many different shapes, sizes, and combinations. For some, holding on to their cultural identity is still important, even if they've relinquished religious dogma. Amy and her family still celebrate Jewish holidays, even though she and her husband no longer believe in God. She shares her views and experiences of important holy days:

My husband and I have always agreed that religious dogma has no place in our family. That said, I still culturally identify as a Jew, so that muddies the waters a bit. My husband was raised Christian, no particular denomination. We both soured on religion in our teens and haven't practiced since. I knew when we had children that I wanted them to understand that they, too, are culturally Jewish. I hang onto this identification not only as a link to my heritage, but also because I cannot ethically disengage from a culture that historically has nearly been obliterated time and again. A professor of mine in college referred to this type of disengagement as finishing Hitler's work. I took that to heart.

In our household, we will sometimes honor Rosh Hashana (the Jewish New Year) with apples for a sweet new year and occasionally we will join friends or extended family for a Passover seder meal, but the one holiday we always celebrate is Hanukkah. Hanukkah is considered a lesser of the Jewish holidays because it commemorates a victorious battle and a small miracle of oil lasting for eight days. It is not a particularly holy holiday. This holiday occurs during the Christmas season, so Jews now celebrate it with gifts. We light the menorah—the candelabra with eight arms for candles representing the eight days of oil, and a ninth arm, usually higher than the rest to hold the Shamash candle, the one that lights the rest. During Hanukkah, my two kids finish their dinners quickly so that we can light the candles at sundown, which is tradition. After I sing the prayer over the candles, each of my kids is allowed to open one small gift. Usually, my extended family—my sister, brothers, and my father, my niece and nephews—will gather during a weekend night of Hanukkah to eat a heavy meal of traditional Hanukkah food: potato pancakes (latkes) with applesauce and sour cream, noodle pudding with cream cheese and raisins (kugel), and maybe some donuts (sufganiyot). Yes, we'll also have vegetables and salad, but the fried foods are symbolic of the miraculous oil, so we must include those in the meal and my non-Jewish husband has become the chief latke chef. Because most of the Hanukkah celebration revolves around food and gifts, maybe the occasional spin of the dreidel, which my kids love bringing for show-and-tell at school, we don't run into much trouble over religious contradictions. Even the prayers are in Hebrew, so it feels more ritualistic than religious. My father and siblings know we aren't religious and, for the most part, none of them are, either.

Christmas is a little bit of a different story, as is Easter. We have a Christmas tradition in my immediate family, one with which I am satisfied. On Christmas Eve, we go to my in-laws' house for dinner and gifts. On Christmas morning, we make a big breakfast, invite over a friend who has become my kids' adopted nana, and we all stay in our pajamas and open presents. For Easter, we hide eggs and put candy in what my husband calls "Spring Baskets" and I jokingly call "Secular Humanist Baskets." This past year, the "eggs" had a Star Wars theme, Darth Vader and Yoda heads filled with jelly beans. It felt less religious, more festive. My in-laws are practicing Christians, as are my husband's sister, her family, other nieces, nephews, cousins, and aunts. Attending Christmas dinner or Easter lunch with this large group of Christians is often a little unsettling for me, but only during the few minutes before the meal. This is when the assembled crowd joins hands in a circle and prays with eyes closed to Jesus, Jesus, and Jesus. I usually head to another room to wait out the prayer, so as to be respectful. Lately, my kids have decided to join me in the other room. My nine-year-old daughter told me a year ago that she prefers to be with me. She also identifies—along with her dad—as agnostic. I'm not sure she knows what it means, but she's very skeptical—never believed in the Tooth Fairy or Santa Claus—so I'm betting she does.

Perspective from an
Ex–Jehovah's Witness

S usan was a Jehovah's Witness (JW) for twenty years before becoming an atheist. There are almost eight million JW members worldwide. They don't observe Christmas, Easter, or birthdays, believing that the celebrations have roots in pagan traditions. Susan wrote that she felt a tremendous sense of freedom and relief after abandoning her religion:

> *Those who belong to the JW faith don't vote or observe national holidays, salute the flag, or join the military because their hope is in God's kingdom and it is considered a form of disloyalty to put their allegiance in human governments, which are controlled by Satan and slated for destruction. It's a bit more complicated in that they may vote for local issues, like school levies, but not for leaders who set themselves up in the place of Jesus. Most won't even vote for the issues, as their consciences won't let them.*

JW are not allowed to celebrate the Christmas season with any type of decorations, secular or otherwise:

I have watched ex-Jehovah's Witnesses struggle to make Christmas special for their children, but they have no real reference point if they were raised in the religion. So they make it as special as possible. Ex-JWs can really go overboard at Christmas. That's the biggie—Christmas. When that time comes, they will become obsessed with it. They will post pictures of their highly decorated homes, and post music and art. Once we celebrate the dreaded, evil Christmas, it really means we are truly free. It's a statement, and the celebration has as much to do with freedom as the holiday.

Another atheist agnostic mother of four daughters (all previously Jehovah's Witnesses) shared this:

Commercialism is something we've struggled to find a balance with. We really try to limit the gifts so that the kids appreciate the spirit and the value of time spent together as a family. They are actually really cute about it—even if they have a dozen gifts waiting, they open one, play with it, spend time with it. They don't rush from gift to gift. So hopefully we are succeeding in making it a special time for them for the right reasons. It's one of the main reasons we've been trying to develop a Christmas tradition.

I just wanted to add that although we are somewhat indifferent to most holidays, the one we've really embraced is Halloween. We have great fun with it, and the grandkids just love planning their costumes and dressing up. I think it's because Halloween doesn't pretend to be anything but pagan. With Christmas I think my daughters still have some cognitive dissonance about celebrating, just as many do—the commercialism, loss of true meaning, etc.

Twenty-year-old Dave was forced to leave home when he came out as gay. Though he misses his family, he noted that the holidays are surprisingly fun and "tend to bring people closer together. You really get to know someone more intimately and well at these times. The JWs don't tell you that." Although celebrations don't have much significance for him, having been raised not to acknowledge them, Dave found many traditions that the JWs demonize, like Easter egg coloring and even celebrating a birthday, enjoyable.

Those who leave the faith are almost always shunned by family, friends, and community members. Not only do they lose their religion, they also lose their support system and those they love. There are nonbelievers who are still practicing Jehovah's Witnesses. The fear of shunning, of being isolated from their families, is so strong that some pretend to believe for their children's sake. One father told me that he loves his kids more than his own temporary happiness. He has spoken with his children about his lack of belief in the religion and has told them why he attends church and pretends. His guise as a believer has allowed him to remain part of his children's lives and has given him the opportunity to share his doubts. They understand that, if he came out of the closet, he would lose contact with them. Yet he does what he can—tries to open a door for doubt and tries to teach critical thinking skills—so that his children can one day be free to choose.

RESOURCES FOR EX–JEHOVAH'S WITNESSES

If you are an ex-JW, here are some resources to help you:

www.jwonline.org: Jehovah's Witness support forum.

www.jwfacts.com:

Excellent resource for those who want to learn

the facts about the JW faith, past and present.

www.atheistgeeknews.com:

A forum run by a JW turned atheist.

www.silentlambs.com:

For those JW who were sexually abused.

· IN THE · COMMUNITY

God in the
Doctor's Office

For a short while, I went to a general practitioner who had Bibles scattered throughout his waiting room. There were very few magazines, but a lot of religious paraphernalia. Yet it's the pictures that hung on the walls that troubled me. They were of a doctor performing his duties—reading a medical manual, examining patients—and behind the doctor was Jesus. (Of course, he was the typical hippie white guy with flowing robes.) It's a little creepy to think that a two-thousand-year-old man is watching over your doctor's shoulder, but it got me wondering, What if Jesus isn't there the day I bring my kid in really sick and my doctor misses something? Surely God's son cannot be in this one office for each and every patient all day long, all year long. He's got to take potty breaks and vacations. How would our savior decide where to be and when? Does he check in only when the patient is a hot chick and leave when it's an old lady on her last legs?

My mother has faced a similar issue with a doctor who tells her that he will pray for her. I'm sure it's a gesture of comfort, but if you're a non-believer or just a private person who feels a little uncomfortable with the intimacy of a stranger praying for you at bedtime, this might be a little awkward. Is a prayer a supplement to or in place of medical treatment? Who knows for sure. But it doesn't give me—or even my mother, who is a believer—a lot of confidence in the doctors who are tag-teaming with the great trinity, that being the Father, Son, and the Holy Ghost.

If finding another doctor is not an option for you because your town is a one-doctor kind of place, or if you think your medical professional might do just fine on his own, you should ask your doctor to leave references to or recruitment for God out of professional conversations. Why do you have a right to do this? Because you *pay* for his services (and that is his, not His, services). There's no mention of God on the HIPAA form you sign for you and your kids, so he should not be in the examination room with you. Maybe you'll even get a price break since you're not paying for the additional expertise.

Of course, the doctor has every right to say no and refuse to provide service, in which case you will know that not only does your doctor need a wingman to practice, he doesn't respect the beliefs and rights of his patients. That doesn't make for good medicine or good healing. Doctors who cannot separate themselves from their imaginary master might have bigger problems than keeping patients.

Remember that now you have more choices—there are medical providers available online and nurse-practitioners in the bigger pharmacies like CVS.

Homeschooling: Keeping Your Opinion to Yourself

was at a well-known sports facility with my sons, and a woman and her two daughters were sitting at the table next to us. She and I were having a nice chat about the sports programs our children were participating in. She mentioned that she was homeschooling her kids, so this place was really convenient for her. I mentioned that she must have a lot of patience, and for that comment, I regret opening my mouth. She then launched into a fifteen-minute sermon about the goodness of God and how he had provided money for her to stay home so she could homeschool. She was interrupted at one point by her young daughter, who said, "Mommy, is this right? 'There shall be no other God before me?'" She paused, then continued her sermon to me, telling me how times were tough for her family but God always found a way for them.

Nothing shuts me down faster than hearing someone say how God loves them so much that he does _____ for them.

"That's nice," I told her and returned to my book.

My older son was sitting beside me, and since he's a teenager, he has his own opinions now. He just rolled his eyes at me. Later he said, "Really? Did that woman really think God was giving her money to homeschool her kids when so many people around the world are hungry?"

The answer, of course, was yes. One of us could have brought this up, told this mom in front of her children how ridiculous it was to think that she and her brood have been hand-picked by God to receive an all-expense-paid religious education at home while people all over the world are in need of basic food, shelter, and medical care. But what good what that have done? She was programmed to think that a big guy in the sky was attending to her needs, was listening to her prayers, and was fiddling with her life.

But her belief was not harming us. We would never have to talk or listen to this person again. Being confrontational only creates ill will between believers and nonbelievers, and it hurts humanity's heart. So unless she was using her God as a club to attack our morality, unless she tried to force her lessons on my kids, I didn't care what crutch she used to get her through the day, through life. Live and let live. It's the Golden Rule again, the rule that should unite us, no matter what we believe about the existence of God.

No, Thanks: The Church Lady at the Gym

'm actually not a bad tennis player—not great, but not bad. So when an acquaintance from the gym tells me she's a longtime tennis player, too, I give her my phone number.

"I'll call you Saturday," she said. Her kids are off to college, and she can play any time, singles or doubles.

Not this weekend, I told her. *My kids have soccer tournaments and piano recitals and friends coming over. No time. What about next weekend?*

But when next weekend comes, she can only play Sunday.

OK, I tell her. *Any time.*

"We go to church Sunday mornings," she says, then enthusiastically adds, "What church do you go to?" She jumped on it so fast that I suspected I had been set up.

I don't, I reluctantly told her. I'm used to people either trying to convert me or giving me the cold shoulder. *I'm agnostic.*

"Oh," she says. "Right. We go to Prestonwood Baptist, and it's a great church. You should try it sometime."

Hmm, I say. Apparently, she didn't hear me say *I'm agnostic* (meaning I don't believe in Jesus Christ, religion, or anything involving wizards, devils, or sprites). Or perhaps, in her church, respecting the beliefs of others is not a topic that comes up for discussion. I know about Prestonwood Baptist, and they teach their followers to evangelize; they make it critical for salvation. She follows behind me, a walking advertisement, rattling off all the different opportunities to get involved in Bible studies and women's groups, telling me about the size of the church and its many amenities. I wondered how much it must cost to support such a big operation.

You should try agnosticism. Then you could play tennis on Sunday mornings, I want to tell her, but don't. It would either offend her or shift her into attack mode, and I'd be engaging in the behavior I tell my kids to avoid.

Sounds nice. But I'm not interested in attending church, I tell her instead.

Of course, she never called. Maybe she went home and looked up the word *agnostic*.

Other Awkward Situations
in Our Communities

t's never easy when we find ourselves having to explain that, not
only do we swim in a different direction than many folks in our
communities, we don't even swim in the same stream. One of the
biggest frustrations for many of us is just that everyone assumes we
believe the way they do. It's like assuming that everyone's favorite food
is sauerkraut. An even bigger frustration is that sharing our views can
affect how people treat us. Sometimes they refuse to let their kids hang
with ours; sometimes they give us the proverbial cold shoulder or shut
us out. Our revelations can mean more isolation for us, especially if we
live in certain areas of the country.

Julie had her awkward moment at a small dinner party:

*When I was chatting with the gal next to me, the subject
came up of what books we had read recently. She mentioned
The Shack and how much she liked it. She talked about
how inspiring it was to read and how great the writer was.
I commented that I didn't care for it—the book didn't make*

*sense to me. I told her it was quite far-fetched, and that I
didn't believe in any of that stuff. I'm pretty sure I had had
a couple of glasses of wine by then and felt relaxed enough
to give my review on the book. It's unfortunate I couldn't
recommend some better reading for her that wouldn't have
prompted her to take offense. Since then, when we happen
to bump into one another, we are cordial—a quick "Hi, how
are you doing?"—but we never take the time to visit. Funny
how when people find out you are not religious, they aren't as
accepting as we nonbelievers are of them—mostly because we
have to be or we wouldn't have a single friend. But what kind
of friendship do you have if you can't be your true self?*

Doug is also raising his children without religion. He and his family
lived for a short time in the South, after having lived in the Northeast:

*We moved to western South Carolina a number of years ago
for a business opportunity. At one of the first social events
we attended, we were immediately and pointedly asked by
the wife of one of my new associates, "And what church do
you attend?" Clearly, this parochial Bible-Belter needed to
know where to pigeonhole us in her strict social hierarchy:
Episcopalians on top, followed in order by Methodists,
Baptists, other Protestants, and way, way down the list
Catholics, Jews, and African-Americans and other dark-
skinned minorities of any religion. "None" was all I said to
her. I didn't stay in the Bible Belt for long.*

Jody, who lives in Pennsylvania and is raising two kids without God, shared this:

> *I took my kids to a dentist appointment this week. The hygienist was filling out a school form for my older son, and when she asked his middle name, she commented, "Oh that's wonderfully biblical. You are so blessed." My son's name, while perhaps sounding biblical to a Christian, is not. He is named after family members. I had a moment of hackles-up defensiveness, then had to take a deep breath and let it go. It was a conscious choice on my part to say nothing. This particular hygienist has been so fantastic with my dentist-phobic son that I decided it wasn't worth the risk of having her treat him/us differently. But, yes, it seems to be a struggle on a daily basis to deal with Christians' assumptions that we are all like them, and we want to chat about religion in casual conversation.*

Many nonbelievers take this nonconfrontational approach. We have to know when to speak up and when not to. Every day we encounter these situations with family, friends, and strangers. Jody took the high road—a deep breath in and tolerance out. We've already learned as nonbelievers how to coexist with our religious neighbors.

Not everyone is ready to coexist with us, however. A reader from Texas wrote:

> *I believe in God, and I also believe Satan is at war with Him. There will always be a war until God puts an end to it in accordance with what's been written in the Bible in the book of Revelation. When I see the bumper stickers that say "Coexist," I realize that there are very naïve people out there. False religions cannot coexist with the one true God.*

A Hero at the Car Wash

Heroes can be found in the most unlikely places.

Like the car wash.

When we think of what makes a person a hero, we think of brave one-time acts, such as rescuing a child from a burning building. Usually, the hero has acted on impulse to save someone, which begs the age-old question: If a person doesn't think about what he is doing, hasn't consciously chosen that action, is he truly a hero?

Last week, as I was waiting at the car wash, a mother came in with two young boys and sat at one of the small tables in the waiting area. One son was reading quietly; the other son was playing with an action figure. Every once in a while, the boy with the action figure would yell and pound the table.

A few of the other customers stared. One older woman shook her head and left to wait outside. No doubt, they thought the child was just misbehaving.

The kid, probably ten years old, continued having outbursts. Yet the mother never got angry. When he seemed particularly frustrated with his toy, she pulled him to her and hugged him. He was clenching his teeth. Then he bit her.

"No biting," she said calmly, though clearly stunned. "No biting," she repeated. He yelled out again. "Quiet voice," she said.

She tried to use sign language to reach him. He was not there. It must be incredibly difficult to raise a child you cannot relate to or communicate with. Being a mom myself, I know you spend nine months rubbing your belly, hoping (or praying, if you're a believer) the baby inside will turn out healthy, inside and out. You hope this for the baby, but also for yourself and your partner, and for siblings, present and future. I had admiration for this mom who didn't get her wish—or prayer—answered as most moms do. Yet she was patient and loving and calm, even through the stares and mean looks; I wanted to reach out, to let her know that not everyone misunderstood.

You are a great mom, I told her before I left. She looked startled.

"Thank you so much," she said. "It's so good to hear that. My husband of eighteen years left me because of this." She looked toward her son. She was raw, injured. If she was bitter that she was left to raise two boys alone, one of them autistic, you could not tell. She was putting herself aside to care for her children.

I still think of her, abandoned, raising her boys without recognition or recompense, with one very demanding, special-needs child. Her love and compassion for her children are inspiring. She is a hero. Every day, over and over again.

■

LISA'S STORY: DISABILITY AND GODLESSNESS

Lisa Morguess is raising her seven (yes, seven) children without religion. She offers wonderful insight into life with a child with Down syndrome, and the frustrations of dealing with people who use God as a coping mechanism:

Shortly after I gave birth to my sixth baby almost five years ago, we found out that he has Down syndrome. Although I was forty when I got pregnant, I declined prenatal testing, mainly because I was planning another home birth, which is typically very low-tech and low intervention. Like most people, it didn't occur to me that I had anything to worry about—things like that happen to other people, right? So when we learned that he had Down syndrome, it came as quite a shock, and it rocked us for a while, in large part because although his birth at home went smoothly, he ended up in the hospital within twenty-four hours having major surgery, and spending almost two weeks in the NICU. It was a difficult time for me, and for our whole family.

Right away, I started hearing about God from other people. "Do you have the Lord?" I was asked. "God never gives anyone more than they can handle," I was told. "God gives special babies to special parents," they said. "This is part of God's plan for you," I heard. "God is trying to teach you something here."

But I had abandoned faith and any notion of God years before, and all these comments simply annoyed me. They weren't the least bit helpful, and in my godlessness, I recognized them for what they were: empty platitudes. I realized that this is how believers offer comfort, by reminding me that there was someone out there—someone bigger and stronger than me—who had a plan, and all I needed to do was have faith in that plan, as mysterious as it might be. I realized that this was just the way some

*people try to make sense of the seemingly inexplicable. And I
realized that behind those words of solace, there was also an
unspoken statement: "Thank goodness it's you and not me."*

*Over time, the shock wore off, and the grief over having a
child who was different from what we had expected passed.
It was never hard to love our son, but it took some time to
come to terms with this new path our life as a family had
been set upon. Through blogging about my experiences as a
mother of a baby with Down syndrome, I became acquainted
with many other parents of children with Down syndrome,
and discovered that faith and God play hugely in how many
families deal with disability and difference within their
families—whether because Christianity is so prevalent to
begin with, or if being confronted by a trauma like having
a baby with a lifelong diagnosis just brings out the God in
people as a coping mechanism, I don't know. Either way, I
found myself in a minority as an atheist parent of a child
with Down syndrome.*

*The religious, I have found, seem to have a need to find
divine meaning in things. Many believers in the Down
syndrome parenting community believe that God has
given their child to them—specially chosen—to teach them
some great lesson, or to use as a tool to teach other people
some great lesson. Some believers believe that having a
child with Down syndrome is a special blessing; other
Christians believe it is a punishment inflicted on the
parents for unrepented sins. Some of these views infuriate
me because of the dangerous ignorance they reflect. Some
irritate me for the same reasons that many Christian*

views irritate me—views that have nothing at all to do with disability, but rather a propensity to foist one's beliefs on others.

What I know is that life is random. Accepting the random nature of things can be frightening, but it's also freeing to know that there is no reason for the things that happen; there is no intrinsic meaning or purpose. It is up to me to glean what meaning and value I can. Nobody and no thing is in control behind the scenes—and that realization allows me the freedom to accept my son without the weight of anger at some divine entity for burdening my son with a disability, and without the sense that I am expected to utilize him to get some dogmatic message across to anyone. I advocate for compassion and tolerance because I know that those are qualities that make the world better for everyone—not because I think there is a God who wants me to advocate for those things, and certainly not because I will be rewarded after I die.

Knowing that there is no god means that there is nobody to appeal to to change me or my children or my life—and nobody to feel disappointed in or let down by for the things that happen (or don't happen). I believe that sometimes, in the dance between egg and sperm, in the delicate division of cells and chromosomes, something out of the ordinary happens, and a child like my son results. You play the hand you're dealt; life and parenting themselves provide innumerable opportunities for growth, for reflection, for learning profound lessons; there is no need to attach anything divine to it.

We can take whatever meaning we choose from every single experience we have. My faith lies in science to better understand Down syndrome—and all other disabilities—from a clinical standpoint, so that individual lives might be better lived. My faith lies in humanity, and people's ability to see beyond outward appearances, to embrace diversity, tolerance, compassion, and inclusion.

Lisa blogs about her experiences at www.lisamorguess.com.

Nonbelievers in Government

Those of us on the fringe count and we are growing, so we should have representation in government, too. Politics is not just for those who hang their hat on a religion. Those like us who are nonbelievers should be allowed to emerge from the religious closet, to state honestly how we feel. We should not discriminate against those who do not believe in God any more than we should discriminate against Jews or Catholics or Muslims.

Seven states still have provisions prohibiting atheists from holding office.[7] In Texas, our stance smacks of the Boy Scouts': You can believe in anything you want, as long as you believe in a God. Article 1, Section 4 of the Texas constitution reads, "No religious test shall ever be required as a qualification to any office, or public trust, in this State; nor shall any one be excluded from holding office on account of his religious sentiments, provided he acknowledge the existence of a Supreme Being." Though the U.S. Constitution trumps the state laws, we should work to remove these discriminatory provisions.

We can encourage our kids to get involved now, take them with us

---

[7] http://www.americanhumanist.org/HNN/details/2012-05-unelectable-atheists-us-states-that-prohibit-godless.

to the voting booth. Tell them to run for student government. Get them ready. Nonbelievers deserve the same sort of representation and acceptance as believers are accorded. Our goal is not to push our "godlessness," but to replace emotion-laden politicians who use God as a point of reference. Helping our children develop leadership skills will benefit them as individuals and will help us collectively.

Good leaders are crucial to making changes in microcosms (like schools and neighborhoods) and in macrocosms (like state legislatures and the Congress). Yet very few people are born leaders; it's a skill that most of us learn over time. As children, most of us are taught to blindly obey authority, to value conformity, and to avoid risk. Good leaders understand when authority should not be obeyed and how to work for change without being disrespectful to the people or society being challenged. They listen and communicate well, consider long-term benefits and consequences, and take action rather than foisting responsibility onto the next guy or gal.

Here are some ways to encourage our children to develop leadership skills:

1. Be a good leader among peers by doing the right thing, by setting a good example. If it is discovered that your daughter, who is a great role model as the captain of her volleyball team, is not a believer, she has just illustrated for her teammates that belief does not make a person good or bad, successful or not.

2. Write a letter to the school principal, the mayor, the newspaper editor, or your state legislators. As soon as your children are able to express their views on a topic, encourage them to share those with others. Maybe your child thinks there is too much paper or food waste at school and wants to address this issue with the principal. Encourage kids to come up with their own solutions—

you'll be surprised at how creative they can be on their own. Or maybe your teen has seen a skate park in another city and wants to request one for your town. A letter to the mayor might get the proverbial ball rolling. If your child is concerned about a topic in the news, many newspapers welcome well-written letters from children and teenagers. Composing letters that thoughtfully address issues of the day (as opposed to just rants or complaints) will help children learn how to be spokespeople for their generation and their community.

3. Form a group to support a cause. For example, if there are people in your community or in a neighboring state that have suffered from a natural disaster, kids can rally their peers to donate food, supplies, and/or money for those affected. If there is a lot of trash in the woods behind the school, your child can lead and encourage other students to help clean it up one Saturday morning. Children can start these kinds of activities at any age, though they may need supervision from Mom or Dad, especially younger ones. Don't underestimate the value and impact of a small project on your community and your child. The sense of accomplishment at having rallied peers to help tornado victims will give them the confidence to tackle larger issues while also helping victims feel that even our young people care.

4. Tutor or mentor. Both middle and high school kids can tutor and mentor younger students in their school districts. If your high school student excels in math, after school she can help a younger child who is struggling with the subject. If your seventh-grader loves to read, he can share his enjoyment of reading by becoming a reading buddy to a younger child. Check with your child's school, since many already have programs in place (especially

through organizations like National Honor Society) to match older students with younger ones.

5. Let them see your involvement. If, for example, you are preparing for a board meeting for your Booster Club, let them sit with you as you write out an agenda or a report. Ask for their input about what you will talk about. For example, how should the Booster Club spend this $1,500? Ask them, "What would you do in my position?" Explain to them how new projects are approved and how the rules are made in your organization.

6. Participate in the YMCA's Youth in Government Program, which helps children learn the challenges and complexities of government and politics. This national program provides opportunities, for example, for middle school and high school students to prepare, write, and vet bills; learn legislative procedure; participate in mock trials; and debate their bills in local, state, and national competitions. Encouraging participation in programs like this will help teach our kids how to make a difference and help create the next generation of politically involved citizens. For more information, check out the YMCA's Youth in Government website, www.ymcayg.org, or ask school officials if they participate in the Youth in Government program.

Tithing

M any preachers will tell you that you need to tithe, to share your greenbacks and help "grow God's kingdom." Even if you're not lucky in life, you're still expected to share your income, no matter how hard-pressed you are to pay your bills. Dave Ramsey, the Christian money-management expert and author of several books on personal finance, encourages believers to keep tithing, quoting the Book of Malachi as proof that giving to God can protect you while not giving to God could hurt your financial position. One young single mom talked about being hounded by her Mormon church to tithe, even though the church knew she was struggling. When she deconverted, she was freed from both an emotional and a financial burden.

The business of church is just that: a business. This is a good topic to bring up with our kids. What goods or services are offered by churches? (For example: hope, comfort, community, networking.) Does the one or two days a week that churches are open justify the huge amount of natural resources used to build and maintain them? How are churches sustained? Let your children know that not only do churches receive funding from members, but churches also receive support from all citizens, regardless of their religious beliefs, through special tax treatment and by using taxpayer-funded goods and services. Does this seem fair?

As nonbelievers, we don't have to deal with the guilt of not tithing enough. Instead, we can determine where our money should go, and we can teach our children that they can invest in themselves and in their futures. Early money-management skills and credit sense are key to helping them transition into financially independent adults. Socking away 10 percent or more (I encourage my kids to save 50 percent of what they have, since they don't have a mortgage yet), of Christmas or birthday money and earnings from babysitting and lawn mowing all add up. I also taught my kids early—starting in elementary school—about savings accounts, bonds, and investing. They have invested their money in all three, and my older son now handles all his own finances and investments. Yes, the money adds up over fifteen years, and he will go off to college with comfortable savings. There are fantasy stock market games that your child can participate in—and some schools (including ours) actually offer these market simulations as part of the curriculum.

Another advantage of losing your religion and keeping your money is that you and your family can decide which charities and causes are important to you and how much you want to support them. Kids should also be encouraged to give of their money, possessions, and time. All three are important and, as adults know, getting others to volunteer their time turns out to be one of the most difficult resources to part with in our busy lives. Allow children to pick which organizations they want to donate to, which fund-raisers they want to participate in. (For ideas, I highly recommend SixDegrees.org, founded by Kevin Bacon, also a nonbeliever.) The charities don't have to be nationally known. There are plenty of people around us who need help: families struggling with medical bills, animal rescue groups that need food and supplies. At my younger son's school, students raised money for a peer who had cancer and whose family did not have adequate insurance.

Tell kids the reason they need to reach out in some way: We are responsible for this planet and for the creatures living on it. If there is no God, no angels that come down to help us, we're it. We need to help each other out. It defines our humanity. And there are so many ways to help out, little and big.

LESSONS
LEARNED

Why I Don't Believe

Over the years that I've been blogging, many have asked me why I don't believe. It's not because God didn't help me in my time of need or that he doesn't "talk" to me. I don't feel abandoned, deserted, or betrayed. I don't believe in God, so these issues and feelings are not even relevant. How can I feel betrayed by someone who's not real, who I don't believe exists, who I'm highly suspect ever existed?

Not believing is not some sort of rebellion against the Lord. God just doesn't make sense—I consciously made a choice not to believe, given that there is no evidence of a deity. (The Bible, the Torah, the Koran, the Book of Mormon—none of these are credible for a variety of reasons that nonbeliever readers will already know.) There is no divinely inspired anything on this planet: no books, no stories, no people. There is no proof of the "word of God."

I'm not angry or disappointed with "God." That's silly. I just find nothing convincing in what I was taught for the first sixteen or so years of life. For certain, I find nothing convincing in the God humanity has created, the God we know in the twenty-first century, who has been passed down, adulterated, and been reborn many, many times since humans were first able to conceive of God(s).

Could the Creator be Benjamin Franklin's clockmaker who set the world in motion and then left? Perhaps, but to me, still highly unlikely. If there is any sort of supreme being or force, I cannot perceive it. I cannot find proof here. We've created God in our own image out of need, out of weakness. But he's no longer necessary, and I'm not willing to abdicate my reason and responsibility to an imaginary being. I might as well believe in Casper. Believing in a God requires that I give up the best part of myself—my ability to think logically.

I'm not immortal. I'm not designed to live forever. That's just a fact. Only in our human-centric world are we the reason, the light, the title-holder of every animal, every place. It's only because we're brought up to believe that we live forever that we expect to live forever. But expectations can be dangerous. I have to wonder: Is living with the knowledge that we will one day put our heads down and never awaken worse than the idea that we might be (somehow) transported to a fiery pit of torture to live for all eternity? Is living our entire lives in fear of the Devil and hell a quality life? Is it worse to think that we must devise our own plan, rather than try to figure out what "God's plan" is for us?

The universe? It doesn't care about you or me. It is indifferent. It knows no good or bad or anything in between. It is amoral. There is no such thing as fate. Sh*t doesn't happen for a divine reason. People don't get what they deserve. And sometimes they get more or less than they deserve.

Humans ascribe meaning to everything: to words, to actions, to events. We create history and re-create it. Constantly. We create gods, and we abandon them. We define ourselves and our experiences. As we grow as human beings, we redefine ourselves. We shuffle our memories to fit our personal narratives.

Life is not easy but, as my grandmother said, "Things that are worthwhile are not easy." It takes work, effort, energy—both physical and emotional—to be a member of the human race. To live is to be scarred, to be an open wound. To live is to change, to become a story with a beginning, an end, some crises, trials and errors, epiphanies, resolutions, and, eventually, conclusions.

I am writing my story—you and I are writing ours—and God's not in it.

Let's Think about
This Story a Little

A t some point in our planet's history, before or after or during the era of the dinosaurs, depending on whose story you believe, a lonely God created Adam and Eve, who were considered his children, though God was truly more akin to Dr. Frankenstein, since Adam and Eve were, more appropriately, his creations, being that this was all accomplished without a Mrs.

Unlike most parents who keep their children out of harm's way, covering up electrical sockets, locking cabinets, hiding the knives, God, the creator of every thing and all time, placed his children in a garden with a very shrewd talking snake, a very dangerous reptile who would forever, God already knew, change the world. This snake was smarter than God's own flesh and blood, proving that the old adage, "The acorn doesn't fall far from the tree," is indeed false, or so we think.

When Adam and Eve disobeyed God and became as knowledgeable as the snake (because, after all, they were curious, as all reptiles and humans are, especially young ones), God didn't just put them in time-out or fine them; he cast them out of the garden forever, onto a hostile planet in an indifferent universe. They would live in a world that would eventually be populated with all sorts of deadly plants and dangerous creatures, the most dangerous and destructive among them being the various forms of the hominids.

Shamed and demoralized, Adam and Eve ventured out into the world, which was not like *The Blue Lagoon,* and had sex, creating (to their surprise) smaller-sized Adams, who, in order to continue breeding, would have to find female animals that looked a lot like Eve—if not aesthetically, then at least functionally. I'm not going to get into the rest of that story as I will, no doubt, be burned at stake.

There are those who say, "No, no, no. The creation story is allegorical. Satan took the guise of a snake!" First, let me say, that if I am able to follow the convoluted explanation of how something can be true without being *literally* true (try telling that to your spouse), as some say the Bible is, I will surely be lost when you tell me how this evil fellow, the Devil, was able to turn himself into a snake. (Ah, Lucifer, yet another one of God's failed creations, cast out for eternity due to disappointing behavior.) Second, let me just suggest that no allegory could possibly explain how a loving creator could get so angry that he gave his kids the boot, kicked them out forever and ever, to suffer and die. Talk about strict fathers.

Fast-forward a long time; the inventor and CEO of humankind was still pretty mad. When God started feeling heavy in the heart and desired to forgive his children (except for that scoundrel Lucifer), he sent his only begotten son to save the rest of his kids, including you and me and our kids and grandkids. This son was not begot through the traditional sense, although some of us are highly doubtful about the Immaculate Conception story. But, wait, some theologians say that God begot a son metaphorically speaking. He just declared Jesus as his son. We can accept whichever story we want, but the point is that Jesus was the son of God, darn it.

Then God did the unthinkable; he did what no sane parent on this planet would do: He sacrificed his kid, allowed him to be beaten and tortured, so that the rest of us could . . . What? Become kinder, gentler people? No, no, no. That's not it. He let his own child be killed so that our "souls," that untouchable, invisible thing that leaks from our bodies *only* after we're dead, could be saved, meaning the rest of us, if we behave, can probably go to a happy place, too.

I'm not quite sure about the rules or the objective of God's game. Why did he have to send another flawed human to earth to die for the sins of the two original screwups so that you and I can live eternally? Between the time Adam and Eve were banished from Eden and the time an angry mob killed Jesus, didn't tons of men and women die because Adam and Eve had sinned? Where did those folks go? Couldn't God have just changed his will or updated his laws there in heaven? Old law: We must suffer and die forever. New law: We must suffer and then maybe suffer forever. We now have the option of heaven, hell, or, for some belief systems, purgatory.

This also brings me to another important question: How come we no longer have talking snakes?

Seeds

You already know that I started my kids out in church. *Hypocrite,* you might think. That's sacrilegious. It might seem odd that an agnostic would take her children to church, but I thought I should give my kids a chance to join the ranks of believers, if they were so inclined. Is it fair to force my views on them? Shouldn't I at least provide a palette full of religious ideas and doctrines from which they could choose or reject?

Faith is a funny thing. I don't think you can grow religious belief in brains that haven't been primed for it. Just as you can't grow plants in infertile soil, you can't plant the belief in God if you haven't planted the seed early in a child's life. While a child is still figuring out the world, it's easy to slip in a belief system or two.

But kids grow up to be logical adults (most of the time). If I were to tell you right now that a wizard lives in the attic of your house, I don't think you'd believe me. If I told you that he was preparing a palace—on your own planet—for you to live in after you die, you'd probably think I was nuts. Yet if I told you there was an almighty supreme being, drilled it into your brain from birth, and reinforced it with church, then you'd believe that an invisible being could summon you to heaven after you die.

It would clearly be difficult to convince a religiously virgin adult to believe in God (though, apparently, it's not hard to do if you're in prison). It is much easier to lose your faith as you age than it is to gain faith when you've had none. For this reason, I decided to take my infant sons and baptize them into the church I grew up in, the Catholic Church. On Sundays and holy days, we were sitting on the pews, anesthetized. Yet every Sunday as I sat in church, I felt sick inside, as if I were doing something wrong.

And I was. I was lying to my kids, programming them with beliefs that I didn't believe in. What was I trying to accomplish? Did I just want them to fit into society? Did I want them to have a religion to identify with? Or did I want them to believe, although I could not, in something bigger?

I sent my sons to a Presbyterian preschool. I figured that learning about Jesus was good. I still believe that, although if I were to start all over again, I would simply tell my sons that Jesus was a man, a good man with many good messages. Was he divine? From what I know about the world, it is not likely.

My kids asked a lot of questions about God early on. For several years, I struggled with telling them what I believed; I didn't want to take away their ability to choose. I reasoned that parents who raised their children to believe that one specific religion was the one "true" religion had chosen for their children. Those parents had already limited their children's ability to choose. Would I do the same thing? Would I limit their ability to choose if I taught them that no religion was "true"? That concern, I learned, was unnecessary. I did not have the proof they asked for, did not make up answers to their many questions about how the world started or where we go after we die. I pulled a thread, and they unraveled the rest. I didn't teach them that religion was false. Using logic, they are coming to their own conclusions.

Turning the Other Cheek:
Our Kids Teach Us Lessons, Too

Kids do not hesitate to call their parents out on something they think is wrong.

My kids had to sell $2 bags of popcorn for a school fund-raiser. Two dollars is not much, right? Well, they went from door to door in our neighborhood stuffed with Texas-sized homes and were turned away every time. One guy didn't even bother to open the door; he just yelled "go away." This is pretty frustrating for teens; they don't like the whole idea of selling stuff to strangers anyway, and I don't blame them. But what made the situation worse was that I always told them, when a kid comes to our house to sell for school, we buy something. That kid will remember that an adult helped her out, and we want to support the schools. Now my children were learning about reality—that not everyone shares those views.

So they came home deflated, and, of course, I got really ticked off as a mother that my neighbors wouldn't buy one measly bag of popcorn.

Fine, I said. *When their kids come around to our door, we're not buying anything, either. And I'm telling them why.*

My kids sulked off, talking about how cheap people were in nicer neighborhoods, how in our "old neighborhood," where the houses weren't as nice, people were friendlier. And they may have been onto something about human nature and wealth accumulation.

A few weeks passed before a high school kid came to my door, selling $20 coupon books for his football team. I stood in the doorway and shook my head at him and said, *My kids tried to sell $2 bags of popcorn in this neighborhood last month and not one person would buy. I'm not buying, either.*" I was probably harsher than I should have been, my indignation surfacing in my voice. I promptly shut the door.

My younger son was behind me; he had come downstairs, and I didn't even realize he was listening. When I turned around, he was angry, "Mom, that was mean. You should have bought something from him. It's not his fault."

I know it wasn't, I told him self-righteously. *But he'll go home and tell his parents what I said.*

"No, he won't," my son said. "He'll just remember that you told him no." We argued a little longer. I knew I had set a bad example, had taken out my frustrations on an innocent kid, a kid just like mine who expected an adult to do a nice thing. So I grabbed my wallet and ran after the kid.

"Hurry," my son called after me. I hoped I could catch him in time to change both his memory and my kid's memory of what had just happened.

I found the boy two houses up, where he had just been turned away.

I'm sorry, I told the kid. *I was just frustrated—and that's not your fault. I'll buy one,* he looked relieved, I think. Or perhaps it was just my conscience that was relieved. *But please tell your parents to do the same when kids come to their door.*

"OK. I will," he laughed. And I believed him.

Nag: A Better Way
to Teach a Lesson

There's a fine line between standing up for what's right and being a nag. Having kids, I am acutely aware of this.

The other night we were at Pei Wei, a popular Asian restaurant, and if you've ever been there, you know there's a sign that says, "Please do not have a seat until after you've ordered." Maybe not those exact words, but something similar. This visit, the line was unusually long as people were finally getting out after a week's worth of snow.

We had just ordered our food and were looking for a table. There was a couple behind us lugging a cumbersome baby seat. I saw a man from the end of the line walk into the seating area and put his coat on the last available table and stroll off.

My first thought was perhaps he just hadn't seen the sign. Surely, he would not take a table when there were so many people ahead of him. But of course we know that some folks are just oblivious to the rules of polite society. So I walked over to the table, with my kids in tow, and stood by it. When he saw me, he rushed over and said, "That's my jacket." And I replied, "You're not supposed to get a table until after you've ordered." He replied, "But my jacket is here." He sat down. At this point, my kids were really embarrassed that I'd confronted the guy. They had followed me, thinking there was an open table. Rather than make an even bigger deal out of it, I walked off and waited for another table to open up.

"Mom, why'd you do that?" my son whispered. He was angry.

Because it's not right, I snapped.

"You're *so* embarrassing!" he said.

Not that I haven't heard that one before, but it got me to thinking. Sometimes, it's just better not to point out the obvious. In the grand scheme of things, this guy's selfishness wasn't a big deal. We see it all the time. A much better tactic was, perhaps, just to ask my kids if what the guy was doing was "the right thing to do." I would have conveyed the message much more clearly. Then, too, everyone would have been happy, and I would not be etched into my son's memory as the world's biggest, most embarrassing nag.

Desensitizing
the Next Generation

My son told me yesterday that he thinks more people know we're nonbelievers than I realize. He said some of the kids on his tennis team know, had known for a couple of weeks. I asked him how they found out. CNN.com, he said. One of the girls on the team had read an article online that I wrote about raising kids without religion.

Were they upset? I asked.

"No," he said, *but a few were surprised.* They came up to him and said, *"Your mom is an atheist?!"*

I'm sorry, I said. *I hope that didn't cause problems.* He shrugged his shoulders.

"No, the team knows you. It gave me a chance to tell them, 'My mom doesn't need religion to have good morals.'" If they said anything mean, he spared me.

I was touched. He was growing up, and he had come to his own conclusion that our belief system was OK. But what I was also thinking was this: For three years, I've had the team over to my house for parties, for hanging out. When other families wouldn't step up, I welcomed everyone to my house, fed them, allowed them to spend the night. I got to know those kids, and those kids got to know me—as a person with the same strengths and weaknesses as any other parent.

They learned that there were no animal sacrifices at my house. We don't stay up all night and drink the blood of innocent children. I was a normal-looking parent who said normal things. They came to my house and swam and played pool and volleyball and made good memories.

Young people judge, but not as fast or as harshly as adults. Their minds are still open because they are growing and learning and trying to be different than the generation before them. Who knows if there will be any fallout later with their parents if they find out we're nonbelievers. For now, they have been desensitized a bit, this group of kids in a conservative town. They know a nonbeliever, have known one for a while, and what they've learned is that we've all been getting along just fine.

They will emerge into adulthood and know that nonbelievers live among them, and that's okay, and the status quo of their parents will be shed like the old, outgrown skin of snakes.

Dumb Parents

No doubt, one of the absolute hardest things about parenting is when you see your kids pulling away from you. You sense it before you actually see it. They don't talk to you as much. They tell their friends more than they tell you. They're quiet and sulky where once they were talkative and giggly.

It's a sign of successful parenting that your kids want their independence, that they are capable of caring for themselves. But it is really hard on Mom—and Dad. The kid who once wanted you to go with her to the movies or who looked to you for answers now sees you as her jailer or as her "dumb" parent. It happens to everyone, eventually. You just have to sit back and ride it out. Hopefully, kids will come out on the other side, intact, ready to have a new relationship with you.

Since I believe in wishes, not prayer, I can only wish that my kids stay out of trouble as they move through their teenage years and hope that I've done my job well enough that they know the way without my lead.

Smile

'm warning you now: This is a little corny. But here goes. I'm giving you a big smile.

The reason? Happiness may be contagious. But don't take my word for it—there are medical studies that support this. Data from the Framingham Heart Study[8] found that our happiness is related to the happiness of those around us. Researchers believe that emotional states can be transferred from one person to another, regardless of whether the people know each other. Happiness is catching, and it is my belief that catching happiness is much better than catching a cold, the flu, a stomach virus, or an STD.

The findings from this study ring true for me since I've tried out informal happiness-contagion experiments on people around me, especially my kids. Kids are very attuned to when their parents are happy. Moms already know this. Kids feel Mom's happiness, and they seem to be much more amicable when we're smiling and humming. The saying is true: When Mom is happy, everyone is happy. On the other hand,

---

[8] *British Medical Journal*, http://www.bmj.com/content/337/bmj.a2338.

grumpiness is also catching because I've certainly seen that transfer to my kids before, too.

I thought this would be a topic to address because being happy is one small way little people, like you and me, can spread peace. We don't have to spread the "word of Christ." We just have to smile, and we can spread cheer and goodwill, not only during the holidays but all the time. The smallest gestures sometimes have the biggest impact. What happens if your smile is not returned or is met with a frown? Well, just be glad you don't live with that person.

I'm smiling. I'm glad we're sharing this life experience together.

The Catholic Argument

I have to admit: every once and a while, I hop on over to the other side and read Catholic blogs. It helps cement my beliefs about religion.

A recent post on a Catholic site dealt with abortion. This is what the author wrote:

> *Abortion is the exact same thing as killing a grown man or woman except they cannot yell stop! God has a reason for putting a child on this earth. No one knows the exact reason but whatever it maybe, it is important. For God does not make mistakes; everyone He puts on this earth is meant to have a life. No matter how short or long it is, we cannot destroy it. God cares for each and every individual, so stand up for life! Make God proud of you!!!*

Of course, we don't know why God put the baby in a woman's belly, but he had his reasons. We do know (for a fact) that God really exists and does not make mistakes (even when babies are the result of one-night stands or are born with birth defects). He cares for every individual (even starving children), and he is proud of those (doctor killers) who stand up and selectively call for an end to terminating life (just human, newly conceived "life," that is). After the kid is born, she's on her own.

Those married folks who've been trying for years to make babies? Too bad. God decided you weren't ready, weren't mature enough, or rich enough, or married enough, or Christian enough . . . something. It's not for us to know.

I have to wonder about this: "God has a reason for putting a child on this earth." Reason implies forethought. Baby-making is God's business, right? It doesn't have anything to do with two people dropping their pants and partaking in the usual behavior of animals? If it is God's will, then we're all little puppets, and we can't help what we do or when we do it. We're just conduits. I also wonder, then, why God hasn't put a restraining order on the genitals of some of these people who make for bad parents.

Look: If you're going to convince me that a teenager shouldn't have had an abortion, you need to make a logical argument. I don't believe that "God" was there when she and her partner were getting busy. I don't believe that one fetus should have been saved over that of any other animal's fetus—and it's only our anthropocentrism that has us convinced that we are more important than any other species.

If you believe you must stand up for life, then you cannot discriminate between which animal deserves life and at what point in the life cycle one deserves to live or die (for those who believe in capital punishment or in sending our kids to war). And if you are standing up for a life, you must take responsibility for that life after it's born and until it is able to care for itself.

The fact is there are too many people on earth and way too many bad parents. If you don't have the resources, room, or maturity, I certainly won't judge you for taking your newly germinated seed and disposing of it. Sometimes "accident" or "mistake" is simply the reason.

Failure

As long as you know that God is for you,
it doesn't matter who is against you.

Keep the Faith, God will provide!

God doesn't give us what we can handle,
he helps us handle what we've been given.

Believing in God, any god, just makes life seem so much easier. Take, for example, the words above that I've saved from friends who posted these and many, many more inspirational Godly quotes on Facebook, the unofficial Internet church.

There are times you really wish you could believe all those trite, one-dimensional sayings because some days you sure could use the fantasy of someone else being in this with you—of making you feel as if you're not alone, which we all are, no matter how many kids or friends or wives we have (that's just for those living in Utah).

Some days you just feel like a loser. Because you try to make every-body happy, you make nobody happy. You disappoint everyone, even yourself. You can't get organized, can't get work done. You rush from place to place, always in a hurry, arriving late or leaving early because you've overscheduled (again, trying to make everyone happy). You worry if you're teaching your kids right or enough, if you've spent enough time with them. You worry if you've spent enough time with your spouse or partner. You worry if you've spent enough time with your friends. Maybe you've hurt someone you care about, broken a thing or a heart, offended a neighbor, held onto a grudge, missed something at work, yelled at the kids, forgotten an appointment or dropped the ball on paying a bill. Yeah, I've done them all, and will surely, as part of the human experience, do them all in varying degrees again. (Note that I'm using *you*, but I really mean *me* or maybe even *us*, for there surely must be others who feel this way on certain days.)

There's always someone who needs something; someone you've dis-appointed. You worry because you know that if you fail, it's no one's fault but your own. A fail is a fail no matter how you look at it. It's not part of a larger plan. Sometimes, you're not even aware it's a fail until you hear it come out of someone else's mouth. Like your kid's.

Sure, believers can say "It's God's plan," but that's just a way of making themselves feel better about the bad things, about the fails, that happen in life. Maybe they'll say, "It was fate." And if you don't believe in fate or destiny or any of those other things that require the hand of some great puppeteer, you're just left with flimsy, capricious luck. Or worse: the fallout from a bad decision.

You might be thinking, well, you can't make everyone happy, but the truth is if you're alive and well in society, someone is always counting on you. People need each other, and it's your duty to step up to the plate, whether it's personally or professionally. If you have children, you always have to be on, not just because they need you to do things but because they are always watching and listening to you. You are their guidebook, their bible, their walking radio station and television show of how to live life and what to say. If you are lucky enough to have parents who are still alive, it might be your turn to watch over them as they watched over you, as one day your children, having learned from you, will also care for you.

All that "God is in your corner" or "God is going to help you" self-talk just gets you from point A to point B. While some folks think it's God helping, you and I know that we make our own decisions and choose our reactions in the face of life's challenges. But, hell, wouldn't it take a little of the burden off to know that someone all-powerful and all-knowing is pulling for you, that someone is helping you, inside your lonely head, with your burdens?

So I guess there's another thing I need to add to the long list of "What to Teach the Kids." Living with uncertainty is certainly a must, and so is living with and bouncing back from failures, big and small. It's part of the price we pay for life on this planet.

Separation Anxiety

My older son has played varsity tennis since the ninth grade. Every spring, his team goes to a tennis tournament five hours away and spends three days there. The first year he left, it was the beginning of the letting-go process. He was happy to go; he needed the break, he said—needed the break from his brother and from school. But I know, even though we're close and he's a really good kid, that he needed a break from me. It's time.

It's time for him to start pulling away and making a life of his own. I was not really ready to let go that first year, but how terribly unfair it would have been to hold him back. As he was heading out the door, I bit my lip and held back the tears. The last thing I wanted was for him to see me getting upset. Now, in his senior year, I don't feel as sad that he is going away again; I just feel sad that soon our home will not be his home.

The thing is, little girls grow up, but they still come back and they still talk to their moms. Boys grow up and grow away. They find a mate. They stop confiding in you. Girls take care of their mothers, and they become friends and confidantes. Boys just leave. I know that's stereotyping, but it's all I've ever seen with all the boys and men in my life.

So this is one of the jobs I have: to parent and then to liberate. Soon, though I'll always be a mother, I'll be retiring from my most important, difficult, and rewarding job as a parent. But, that's OK. The finished product has turned out well enough to release to the world. My son's way more focused than I ever was at his age. He makes good grades without any threats from me. He does the right thing most of the time. When he has the chance to spend or save, he saves. And he's respectful, even when I'm demanding. He's not afraid to tell me, gently, when he thinks I'm wrong. And he apologizes when he's wrong. I think it's OK to let go now.

Win-Win

"**G**od has decided this is what's right for you. He's given you other gifts." This is what a parent told me yesterday. She wasn't talking about me. She was talking about her son and what her preacher had said.

Her kid was too short. For her, at least. He's at that awkward age where the boys and girls start to grow a lot. But her son was still small, and he wanted to play basketball. His short stature, she claimed, was the reason he didn't make the team. *He'll grow,* I told her. *Some boys grow late. He's only in middle school.*

"No, he'll be short like me," she said.

She told me that her son had not told his friends he didn't make the team. He was too embarrassed. I wondered why. I'm sure it had nothing to do with the fact that his mother would tell complete strangers that her son wasn't growing to her liking.

I also wondered if God was up there somewhere, doling out height cards as gifts for newborns. When he ran out of height cards, he passed out the brains, then the good looks. Which gift was considered most valuable?

The funny thing is this: The Christian God is always in a win-win situation. If something is not to your liking, no worries. It was God's plan, and there is something else he wants for you (keep looking and keep praising the Lord). And if you have a blessedly perfect life, that was God's plan, too. It was meant to be—keep praising the Lord so you keep it.

Is there any other person, real or imagined, who has it so good?

Why I Don't Take
Rejection Personally

I normally like to take credit for what I say, but I blogged anonymously on the topic of raising kids without religion for many years for the simple reason that people—at least where I live—are not very accepting of those who don't believe in their God. I live in a very religious area with a lot of Baptists and Mormons. Although there seem to be more people questioning religion these days, there are still a lot of people who harbor prejudice against nonbelievers. The belief is that there's something wrong with you if you don't worship a deity—or worse: You're one of those amoral people who will be heading down to the deep, hot South in the afterlife.

I know for certain that two women I used to be friends with are no longer friends with me because they know I don't go to church. They are still polite, but they won't let our kids hang out together any more. I feel their distance. And that's OK, I suppose. I could say that a real friend doesn't turn her back on you because you believe differently than she does. But that's too simple. Friends, like people who marry, want to share common belief systems. It's awfully hard to rise above religious differences, especially when your religious convictions are supposed to be shared with others. What do you say to your agnostic friend when she sneezes or when she is struggling with sorrow?

When we come out of religion's closet, we may just find that this leaves those of us who don't believe in God with a smaller group of friends to choose from; although, perhaps this is just natural selection at work. People naturally choose to surround themselves with friends who think the way they do—not always, but most of the time. I guess it works the other way, too. It's hard to pretend you're a believer when you're not. And, of course, I want my friends to know me—that I'm capable of being a good friend even though I'm not a Christian as they are.

So I understand why some people don't want to be friends. I don't take it personally.

God Bless You and Other Things We're Not Supposed to Say

I curse. I say *Goddamnit* when I notice the dog peed on the floor (again). I say *Jesus Christ* when I stub my little toe on the bed (again). I say *God Bless You* to a stranger. I tell myself it is silly to say these things. Like goose bumps, a vestigial behavior that is no longer necessary, I use vestigial language. God references remain a reflex to me. When I hear a sneeze, *God Bless You* pops out, although I know I don't mean it in its traditional or more literal sense. I just seem to want to communicate to another human being that, *Hey, I know bad things are supposed to happen to you physically and spiritually when you sneeze, and I just want you to know: I don't want that happening to you.* I could say *Gesundheit,* as I occasionally heard my dear old dad say, but that just doesn't get the meaning across in America like a good old-fashioned, *God Bless You.* Besides, *gesundheit* sounds like something that comes *out* of your nose when you sneeze, and I'm not talking about your spirit.

As for why I curse God, I'm not sure. It seems as if I would have substituted the f-bomb instead. I suppose that, being brought up Catholic, nothing sounds quite as impressive as *goddamnit*. Only now I don't need to go to confession for taking God's name in vain. (Sorry, Mom.)

On the other hand, I also thank God. I say *Thank God* a lot, meaning, I thank whatever forces may be at work: Lady Luck, Mother Nature, and Ms. Fortune (not, misfortune), whom Machiavelli identified in *The Prince* as "always, womanlike."

I also say *Oh my God!* (*OMG!* for the younger ones). I use that expression a lot. I don't know why, since it means nothing to me, but I can't break the habit. I notice that my kids use this expression, too, which they most likely picked up from me. Or school. Or both. Once, while I was talking with my mother, an OMG! slipped out. She stopped talking and asked, "Why do you say that?"

What? I asked.

"Oh my God. You don't even believe in God." I told her it was just a habit—one I've had forever. Why, I wondered, was she making a big deal out of it now? "God wouldn't listen to you," she said.

My sweet little Italian mother, whom I don't look or act much like, had been disappointed in me. I wish she would have brought this up earlier. I would have told her then what I told her that night. *I'm sorry, Mom.* And I was. I didn't follow her lead. Yet I did not want to pretend. I thought being honest was better than lying to her. But it was only better for me—not for her.

In all fairness, as my mother pointed out, not being part of the religious realm any longer, I really shouldn't borrow their stuff. I'm going to *try* to change my ways (Oh my Glob!), the key word being, of course, *try*. Old habits are hard to break. Bad habits are even harder to break. And I want you to know, just in case you're wondering, I don't curse in front of the kids. Some things are still sacred.

Dress Rehearsal

When you don't believe in God and an afterlife, there is no dress rehearsal. This is the real thing. I wake up every morning, and as I'm walking my dog in the dark, I think how this could be the last walk I ever take. Not one minute should be wasted on foolish things. Every morning I give my kids hugs and kind words because I want to, not because I am trying to imitate someone or because I'm trying to earn brownie points, but because they need my love and I want to show it.

When I believed in a God, I put my concerns in the invisible hands of an imaginary person. That removed some of my responsibility but also took away the urgency and the intensity of living. Any mistake here, any deficiency in this life, could be fixed there, addressed later. No matter what happened, it was of little consequence because there was my other life—a better life—waiting in heaven. This was all just a dress rehearsal, so nothing really mattered.

My son went to church last week and, as usual, I asked him about the sermon when he returned. The message was, he told me, that you should not fill empty spaces in your life—those holes left from a divorce or a job loss—with bad habits, like drinking or gambling. That time should be devoted to building a relationship with God, for though this life here isn't perfect, we will be rewarded with a perfect life in the hereafter. This is the crux of what separates believers from nonbelievers: We navigate our own lives and hold tight to those around us; believers follow the lead of their sky pilots and hold tight to hope and promises and visions.

In the big picture, the one we don't like to look at because it makes us feel little and hopeless and powerless, nothing is that important. You and I and our religious neighbors will slip unnoticed by humanity into the ground one day. A few family and friends will miss us, but the people who knew us will die off, too. One day even the last of humanity may die, along with the sun and our planet. Not only is this our only performance, it may be our final performance.

Rivers: Why We Should Embrace Our Neighbors

I t doesn't matter where we came from. One day, you and I just appeared. We were made from the food our mothers ate and the water they drank. We had the same blueprints but with different color variations. We both received hearts and brains and hands to help others with. We were given names. We may speak different languages and listen to different music, but we say the same things and dance to the same rhythms. A smile means the same thing to you as it does to me. We breathe the same air that ancient Egyptians breathed; we drink the same water that dinosaurs drank. If you believe that we all came from Adam and Eve, then you are my blood relative. We live in different houses, but we are connected.

It doesn't matter where we came from or what religion we believe in—or don't believe in; we will all slowly fade away. It will start with the eyes. The words that were once easy to read will become fuzzy and difficult to see. We won't be able to see the imperfections on the faces of loved ones. The hearing will fade. Sounds we could once hear clearly will be completely beyond our ability to hear. Our hair color will fade—maybe even our hair. Our muscles will shrink, and wrinkles will appear on our skin. Our eyes will sink deeper into our heads and our memories will fade, no matter how badly we want to hold on.

Our bodies came from the same place, the same planet, and our bodies will go back to the same place. You. Me. Our children. The short space in between, the small slice of time—our lifetime—is serendipity. It is our good fortune. It's our celebration. Sandwiched on either side of our lifetime is darkness, eternal sleep.

Our religion, our nationality, and our clothes are merely the garments we wear to the party. One day, they'll fade away, too, as our bodies go back into the earth we were created from. Then you and I will no longer be separate islands, but entwined as part of the same river once again.

Understanding

understand the need for religion. It has many benefits. I'm not suggesting that it go away; only that we accept and recognize the benefits of raising children without it, and that we keep our thoughts about God's existence (or nonexistence) out of our schools and public spaces.

Religion itself is not necessarily bad. Religious affiliation provides people with a community of similar hopes, beliefs, and support. A man dying of cancer finds comfort in his church. Parents who have lost a child find answers in a preacher's kind words.

Fears are quelled in church—our fears of our own mortality, of the unknown, of never seeing our loved ones again. In the pews believers find relief for those aspects of life that cause them the greatest dread. They can hand over their problems to someone else. When some believers are confronted with a problem that is too scary or too overwhelming for them, they will often say, "I just prayed and placed my faith in God." They no longer own their problem and its outcome. God does. Sometimes, this is a good thing. We don't always have control over what happens anyway, and praying is just hoping for a specific outcome. But God always wins. If a prayer is answered, then God gets credit. If a prayer is not answered, then it was not God's desire for you. He's a lucky guy either way. And he's always right.

Sometimes, though, offering up our prayers to God means we've abdicated our right to choose. We could effect a change in our choices, but the dilemma is too daunting. So we pray instead and hand over our decision-making ability to an unseen, unknown entity. In other words, some believers just don't make any decision; they allow chance and time to choose for them.

Religion also gives us hope. It's not easy dealing with the fact that each of us, along with the parents and children we love so dearly, will one day cease to exist. Our mortality looms over us like a giant boulder about to drop on our heads. Churches give believers a carrot, a second life to hope and strive for after we're crushed dead on this planet. The goal is heaven; the path is clear. Be a good follower and you will be rewarded. Any imperfection here will be compensated for there. Our sinfulness will be forgiven, and we will live an eternity in the pure goodness of God with everyone we've ever loved. Who wouldn't want that?

There is another upside to religion. Churches do good things: They feed the poor, minister to the sick, and provide comfort for the broken-hearted. But by no means are these good deeds done altruistically or self-lessly. It is not altruism if you are getting something in return, whether it's recognition or a ticket to heaven. Good deeds performed within the context of religion always have a driving force: the promise of salvation. If you think God will smile upon you when you do a good deed, then it is a good deed but also a selfish act. It may have outcomes that benefit others, but it also benefits the believer.

None of these things has anything to do with morality. In fact, most religions teach a diluted form of ethics. They teach children to do the right things (for example, to be honest) for the wrong reasons (God is watching). If you only behave because an invisible man in the sky is watching, then you don't own your own moral structure. Your moral framework is based outside yourself, separate from your reasoning.

A mom from Dallas wrote, "The fact that religions think that you can only be good or moral if you believe in God makes me so mad. Someone once said, 'Character is who you are when no one is watching.' I guess Christians don't know what true character is since God is always watching. I consider myself a very moral person and a good person. I am agnostic. I know right from wrong, not because of religion, but because I am a human being and I know you shouldn't do anything to intentionally hurt someone else. However, I also can allow reason and logic to play a role. In life, not everything is black and white. There are always gray areas. Sometimes, there are no winners and you just have to do what you think is best."

We don't need God or religion to be moral. Yet if religion is what it takes for some people to stay the course, to do the right thing, then I want religion to stick around as long as humanity needs it.

Last Words
from the Cross

Then said Jesus, Father, forgive them; for they know not what
they do. And they parted his raiment, and cast lots.

—Luke 23:34

It's not right for the Christian majority to push their beliefs on nonbelievers, for them to assume that their way is the right way or the only way. You and I know this. But look how far we've come. We are no longer shot, whipped, drowned, or hanged for being heathens. We're making strides, though it may not seem like it some days. You're reading this book; our numbers are growing; people are listening. A mean stare or a few harsh words is nothing like imprisonment.

Any time we, as nonconformists, push back against tradition or against the status quo, we're going to meet resistance. Do we want to be labeled as loud, obnoxious nonbelievers? I don't want to be like that or for my kids to be like that, like the pushy evangelicals who've crossed our

path. I also don't want to take away someone's comfort or their preference for Heinz, Crest, or Christ. When my neighbors or friends think of
atheists or agnostics, I want them to remember that they know someone
who is kind, not belligerent or demeaning. I don't want to force my views
on anyone, just as I don't want their views forced on me. I want to make
my kids proud, my family proud, you proud. You're counting on me, and
I'm counting on you to be a good representative for nonbelievers. Like
systematic desensitization, we can help believers overcome their anxiety
or irrational fears of nonbelievers through positive experiences with us.
That will help, just as knowing someone who is gay has helped the homosexual community gain acceptance in America.

So you and I can continue our conversations, but when we speak
with believers, let's speak softly and reasonably. Let's remain quiet when
we need to and not provoke confrontation. Let's stick together without
ganging up. Say *No, thank you, I don't wish to participate* and *Yes, please,
take your prayer group to your church or home.* We won't be manipulated by fear or hope. One story about how wonderful God is is okay. But
we draw the line at evangelizing. After all, we would not tell believers how
wonderful our dog or kid or spouse is over and over and over again. We
get the idea, and we have boundaries—and believers should, too.

We all have to have our own awakening. We cannot take away
people's religion—they have to give it up. We cannot make the religious
examine the veracity of their ideas because many prefer comfort and
security to scrutiny and reason. But you can see, from the number of
people leaving the church, that we are in the midst of an exodus. Once followers no longer have the reinforcement of religion, of attending a church
with a preacher who tells them what to think and how to behave, they
will start creating their own narratives and God will fall by the wayside.
As our children grow and they have children, our numbers will grow, too.

Some say this is too soft an approach or, perhaps, even too cow-
ardly. But what is our option? Confrontation? Anger? Should we confirm

the fears of some who say we are at war with religion? There is no need for fighting, for it is against what we stand for. We stand for a kind and peaceful world that does not need superstition or extremists. We all just want a better world for our kids.

As I've said before, I do not want religion to go away. I only want religion to be kept at home or in church, where it belongs. It's a personal effect, like a toothbrush or a pair of shoes. It's not something to be used or worn by strangers. I want my children to be free not to believe and to know that our schools and our government will make decisions based on what is logical, just, and fair—not on what our leaders believe an imaginary God wants.

There was a time we needed freedom *of* religion for our nation. Now we need freedom *from* religion.

Conclusion

Most people will not be like us. Most people will choose to raise their children with some form of religion or belief in God. For now we are outliers, but we are growing in number and one day what anyone believes about the existence of a God will be irrelevant. You and I share the same goals with believers: to raise moral kids. That's our most important contribution to our society—kind, compassionate children.

Our families may not agree with our choices—even our spouses may not agree—but we can stand our ground knowing that we are doing the right thing by raising our children free of religious indoctrination. For me, should my children think and reflect and eventually decide when they are older that they want to become Mormons or Baptists or Muslims, I will gladly accept the choices they've made for themselves. To believe or not to believe will be their choice, not mine. I just could not, in good faith, fill them full of tall tales and hand-me-down stories that didn't make sense, that there was no proof for. I didn't need or want a crutch like that. Religion doesn't make sense to me. Neither does God.

Raising kids without religion means that you and I have to live with a bit of a mess, without knowing a lot of the answers. We have to be comfortable with the idea that we are not special, not saved, and not going anywhere after we die. We're not here for any reason other than the one we invent for ourselves. What gives life meaning? The jar is empty, the mannequin is naked. Fill it, clothe it. Make it yours. Christianity teaches us that we are nothing but sinful, undeserving losers who must behave a certain way, think certain things, and not think about certain things. It is not logical, and it is not fair. Life's too short to live tethered to a belief system like that.

The universe may be indifferent, but we don't have to be. Though we may feel alone in our communities, we are part of a larger force. As LanceT, a regular commenter on my blog, wrote:

I see a pattern where the randomness of human actions can be directed through probability for an overall cumulative and positive effect. All throughout our society there is a butterfly effect that we are most always oblivious to . . . I guess my message is to go boldly forth and increase the peace and love and know you are not alone. You may not always be aware of the others choosing to follow this same path as you, but they're out there, and they're making a difference.

I hope you feel less alone. I hope you will stay the course in raising your kids free of religion and God. I'm putting this book out there, just as I'll be putting my kids out there. They'll go off to college and into the world. Maybe they'll become part of organized religion. Maybe they won't. They'll grow and change, unlike this book, which will remain static and unchanged. One day, hopefully, this book will become forgotten because our country has grown and changed around it.

Resources for Nonbelievers

American Atheists: www.atheists.org

American Humanist: www.americanhumanist.org

Atheist Alliance International: www.atheistalliance.org

Atheist Meet-ups: www.atheists.meetup.com

Helping: Foundation Beyond Belief: www.foundationbeyondbelief.org

Helping: Six Degrees: www.sixdegrees.org

The Humanist Resource Connection: www.humanistresources.org

Military Atheists: www.militaryatheists.org

Parenting Beyond Belief, by Dale McGowan (New York: AMACOM, 2007) www.parentingbeyondbelief.com

Recovering from Religion: www.recoveringfromreligion.org

Acknowledgments

I'd like to thank the readers of my blog who graciously shared their stories and experiences, who write with me about raising kids without God and about living as nonbelievers in a predominantly Christian society. We are in this together, seeking freedom from religion for ourselves and our children. I'd like to thank Dale McGowan, who tackled this topic before me and who kindly wrote the foreword for this book. To my dear friend Tracy Carruth, thank you for sharing your wisdom throughout the course of our friendship. I am indebted to Aaron Freeman, who gave me permission to print his beautiful Eulogy. Special thanks to my editor, Kate Zimmermann, for her expertise and for her patience with me as a first-time author.

I am also grateful to my children for their patience through this project and for the many experiences that became material for this book. It's a privilege and an adventure being your mother. To Scott, who has helped me most of all, encouraging me to keep writing and to be myself, my deepest thanks.

Index

About the Author